Perspectives on Children's Spirituality in Diverse and Changing Contexts

This book offers multidisciplinary and inclusive perspectives on children and young people's spirituality and its research in diverse socio-cultural contexts. It brings together a collection of select research articles that were published over a period of nearly two decades (2003–2021) in the *International Journal of Children's Spirituality (IJCS)* to celebrate the journal's 25th anniversary.

Featuring contributions by leading international scholars from the U.K., the U.S., Canada, Finland, Australia, Hong Kong, and China, this edited volume focuses on different and complementary perspectives on children's spirituality in diverse and changing contexts. Chapters cover topics such as the study of children's spirituality as a natural form of human awareness; a proposed pluricultural approach; the potential contributions of psychoanalytic tradition and cognitive psychology; possible influences of tradition(s), multidisciplinarity, and perceptions on understanding children's spiritual experiences; Christian perspectives on children's spirituality in relation to living and dying in Quebec, Canada; Finnish pre-adolescents' perceptions of religion and spirituality; using technology, specifically tablets, as a component for understanding children's spirituality; and cyber spirituality.

This volume will be an invaluable resource for researchers and postgraduate students majoring in education studies, life, and moral and spiritual education and those majoring in psychology and religious studies.

John Chi-Kin Lee is Chair Professor of Curriculum and Instruction, Director of the Centre for Religious and Spirituality Education, and Director of the Academy of Educational Development and Innovation at the Education University of Hong Kong (EdUHK), Hong Kong. He has served as the Changjiang Scholar Chair Professor conferred by the Ministry of Education, the People's Republic of China. Professor Lee is also UNESCO Chair in Regional Education Development and Lifelong Learning at the EdUHK and the Southeast Asian Ministers of Education Organization Research Fellow. He has served as the editor of the *International Journal of Children's Spirituality*, executive editor of *Teaching and Teacher Education*, and editorial board member or advisory editor of many local, regional, and international journals. He is also a prolific writer who has edited and written more than 25 books and published over 100 journal articles and book chapters.

Perspectives on Children's Spirituality in Diverse and Changing Contexts

Edited by
John Chi-Kin Lee

LONDON AND NEW YORK

First published 2025
by Routledge
4 Park Square, Milton Park, Abingdon, Oxon, OX14 4RN

and by Routledge
605 Third Avenue, New York, NY 10158

Routledge is an imprint of the Taylor & Francis Group, an informa business

Preface © 2025 John Chi-Kin Lee

Introduction, Chapters 1,2 and 4–9 © 2025 Taylor & Francis
Chapter 3 © 2019 Kate Adams. Originally published as Open Access.

With the exception of Chapter 3, no part of this book may be reprinted or reproduced or utilised in any form or by any electronic, mechanical, or other means, now known or hereafter invented, including photocopying and recording, or in any information storage or retrieval system, without permission in writing from the publishers. For details on the rights for Chapter 3, please see the chapter's Open Access footnote.

Trademark notice: Product or corporate names may be trademarks or registered trademarks, and are used only for identification and explanation without intent to infringe.

British Library Cataloguing-in-Publication Data
A catalogue record for this book is available from the British Library

ISBN13: 978-1-032-61911-8 (hbk)
ISBN13: 978-1-032-61912-5 (pbk)
ISBN13: 978-1-032-61913-2 (ebk)

DOI: 10.4324/9781032619132

Typeset in Myriad Pro
by codeMantra

Publisher's Note
The publisher accepts responsibility for any inconsistencies that may have arisen during the conversion of this book from journal articles to book chapters, namely the inclusion of journal terminology.

Disclaimer
Every effort has been made to contact copyright holders for their permission to reprint material in this book. The publishers would be grateful to hear from any copyright holder who is not here acknowledged and will undertake to rectify any errors or omissions in future editions of this book.

Contents

Citation Information	vii
Notes on Contributors	ix
Preface	x
John Chi-Kin Lee	

Introduction—Children's spirituality: personal reflections on International Journal of Children's Spirituality (IJCS)   1
John Chi-Kin Lee

1. Investigating children's spirituality: the need for a fruitful hypothesis   9
   David Hay and Rebecca Nye

2. Reviewing the research in children's spirituality (2005–2015): proposing a pluricultural approach   19
   Jennifer Mata-McMahon

3. Navigating the spaces of children's spiritual experiences: influences of tradition(s), multidisciplinarity and perceptions   32
   Kate Adams

4. Living and dying: a window on (Christian) children's spirituality   47
   Elaine Champagne

5. How do Finnish pre-adolescents perceive religion and spirituality?   60
   Martin Ubani and Kirsi Tirri

6. The personae of the spiritual child: taking pictures of the heart using technology and tablets   73
   Kathleen Harris

7. Cyber spirituality: Facebook, Twitter, and the adolescent quest for connection   88
   Karen-Marie Yust, Brendan Hyde and Cathy Ota

8. Cyber spirituality II: virtual reality and spiritual exploration   91
   Karen-Marie Yust, Brendan Hyde and Cathy Ota

9 Shining lights in unexpected corners: new angles on young children's spiritual development   94
   Tony Eaude

   Index   105

Citation Information

The following chapters were originally published in various volumes and issues of the *International Journal of Children's Spirituality*. When citing this material, please use the original page numbering for each article, as follows:

Introduction
Children's spirituality: personal reflections on International Journal of Children's Spirituality (IJCS)
John Chi-Kin Lee
International Journal of Children's Spirituality, volume 26, issue 1–2 (2021), pp. 1–8

Chapter 1
Investigating children's spirituality: The need for a fruitful hypothesis
David Hay and Rebecca Nye
International Journal of Children's Spirituality, volume 1, issue 1 (1996), pp. 6–16

Chapter 2
Reviewing the research in children's spirituality (2005–2015): proposing a pluricultural approach
Jennifer Mata-McMahon
International Journal of Children's Spirituality, volume 21, issue 2 (2016), pp. 140–152

Chapter 3
Navigating the spaces of children's spiritual experiences: influences of tradition(s), multidisciplinarity and perceptions
Kate Adams
International Journal of Children's Spirituality, volume 24, issue 1 (2019), pp. 29–43

Chapter 4
Living and dying: a window on (Christian) children's spirituality
Elaine Champagne
International Journal of Children's Spirituality, volume 13, issue 3 (2008), pp. 253–263

Chapter 5
How do Finnish pre-adolescents perceive religion and spirituality?
Martin Ubani and Kirsi Tirri
International Journal of Children's Spirituality, volume 11, issue 3 (2006), pp. 357–370

Chapter 6
The personae of the spiritual child: taking pictures of the heart using technology and tablets
Kathleen Harris
International Journal of Children's Spirituality, volume 23, issue 3 (2018), pp. 291–305

Chapter 7
Cyber spirituality: Facebook, Twitter, and the adolescent quest for connection
Karen-Marie Yust, Brendan Hyde and Cathy Ota
International Journal of Children's Spirituality, volume 15, issue 4 (2010), pp. 291–293

Chapter 8
Cyber spirituality II: virtual reality and spiritual exploration
Karen-Marie Yust, Brendan Hyde and Cathy Ota
International Journal of Children's Spirituality, volume 16, issue 1 (2011), pp. 1–3

Chapter 9
Shining Lights in Unexpected Corners: New angles on young children's spiritual development
Tony Eaude
International Journal of Children's Spirituality, volume 8, issue 2 (2003), pp. 151–162

For any permission-related enquiries please visit:
http://www.tandfonline.com/page/help/permissions

Notes on Contributors

Kate Adams, School of Education, Leeds Trinity University, UK.

Elaine Champagne, Faculté de théologie et de sciences religieuses, Université Laval, Québec, Canada.

John Chi-Kin Lee, Centre for Religious and Spirituality Education; Academy of Educational Development and Innovation, The Education University of Hong Kong (EdUHK), Hong Kong.

Tony Eaude, University of Oxford, UK.

Kathleen Harris, School of Education and Applied Social Sciences, Seton Hill University, Greensburg, USA.

David Hay, University of Aberdeen, UK.

Brendan Hyde, Faculty of Arts and Education, Deakin University, Melbourne Burwood Campus, Australia.

Jennifer Mata-McMahon, Department of Education, University of Maryland, Baltimore County, USA.

Rebecca Nye, The Open University, UK.

Cathy Ota, Living Well Dying Well Ltd., East Sussex, UK.

Kirsi Tirri, Department of Education Learning, Culture & Interventions (LECI), University of Helsinki, Finland.

Martin Ubani, School of Applied Educational Science and Teacher Education, University of Eastern Finland, Finland.

Karen-Marie Yust, Department of Christian Education, Union Presbyterian Seminary, USA.

Preface

John Chi-Kin Lee

Children's spirituality could be considered as important multidisciplinary or interdisciplinary area of study which connects with spiritual and life, values, and religious education on the one hand and has association with religious studies, philosophy of education, and psychological studies of children on the other hand.

As an established international journal, the *International Journal of Children's Spirituality* (*IJCS*) has been accepted into lots of databases, including the Arts & Humanities Citation Index® (www.tandfonline.com/toc/cijc20/current). The *IJCS* presents a comprehensive definition of spirituality, life, and values education. The journal acknowledges that spirituality, life, and spiritual values can be perceived from both religious and non-religious viewpoints. Furthermore, these concepts can be expressed and analyzed in non-religious settings and within various religious, philosophical, psychological, and sociocultural traditions. (www.tandfonline.com/toc/cijc20/current; Lee, 2020a, 2020b).

This is a companion to *Spiritual, Life and Values Education for Children* published by Taylor & Francis, which represents a special collection of editorials and selected papers from the *International Journal of Children Spirituality* (*IJCS*) which I am honored to assume the role of editorship since 2020. I am deeply grateful for the support by Shreya Bajpai Commissioning Editor, Taylor & Francis, which has made these books possible for publication. In addition to the editorial board members, reviewers, and contributors to *IJCS*, I am indebted to Mr Tony Eaude, Book Review Editor, who has provided a lot of support and advice. I would also like to extend my sincere thanks to Ms Abi Amey and Nasreen Banu who have worked with me in producing the volumes of *IJCS*. When *IJCS* was established, one of the editorials (1996, p. 5) wrote that

> (w)hen considering the issue of children's spirituality such a lack of communication between different practitioners will result in the failure of any initiative. The journal identifies itself as a means of encouraging debate across these cultures as well as across the culture of childhood and adulthood, nationhood, ethnicity and religious identity.

This book will cover the topics, authored by international scholars from various countries (the U.K., the U.S., Canada, Finland, Australia, Hong Kong SAR, and China), such as the study of children's spirituality as a natural form of human awareness (by David Hay and Rebecca Nye 1996); a proposed pluricultural approach (by Jennifer Mata-McMahon 2016); the potential contributions of psychoanalytic tradition and cognitive psychology (by Tony Eaude 2003); and possible influences of tradition(s), multidisciplinarity, and perceptions on understanding children's spiritual experiences (by Kate Adams 2019). There are papers which explore Christian perspectives (by Elaine Champagne 2008) on children's spirituality in relation to living and dying in Quebec, Canada, and Finnish pre-adolescents' perceptions of religion and spirituality (by Martin Ubani 2020 and Kirsi Tirri 2006). In addition, there are papers on using technology, specifically tablets, as a component for understanding children's spirituality (by Kathleen I. Harris 2018) and two editorials on cyber spirituality (by Karen-Marie Yust, Brendan Hyde & Cathy Ota 2010 and 2011).

David Hay (1997) draws largely on perspectives and traditions in the U.K. and Europe as well as literature from the U.S. and the East to help us reflect on the notion of spirituality as "holistic awareness" (pp. 9–10). He also argues (p. 14) that there is a lack of cultural context for enhancing contemporary spiritual education. This viewpoint to some extent resonates his later advice that "…the teacher must do is help children become aware of this and reflect on it in the light of the culture of which they are a part" (Hay, 1998, p. 11). Readers may be interested to follow up Hay with Nye (2006)'s book *The Spirit of the Child* (revised edition) where Hay (2006, p. 149) suggests four responsibilities of teachers in nurturing the spirit of the child as follows (adapted): facilitating children to adopt an open mind; exploring various ways of seeing; promoting personal awareness; and enhancing personally awareness of the social and political dimensions of spirituality.

It is, however, notable that there seems to have a lack of consensual definition of spirituality (Adams et al., 2016, p. 762). Adams and others (2016, p. 766) draw upon ideas of Eaude (2005), Eaude (2006) and Goodliff (2013) who make reference to Hay and Nye's (2006, pp. 17–32) concept of relational consciousness which forms part of spirituality. They also highlight the importance of play which could facilitate children to express their spirituality (Adams et al., 2016, p. 767). In addition, Eaude (2018, p. 64) suggests questions such as "Who am I? Where do I fit in? Why am I here?" which are associated with spiritual development. On the other hand, Fisher (2001, p. 100; cited in Hey, 2020, p. 802) adopts a more comprehensive and integrated view of spirituality which encompasses "the physical, mental, emotional, social and vocational" dimensions of health and well-being.

In different societies and educational systems, there are various traditions and approaches to spiritual education through religious education and other forms of values education (Lee, 2020a, 2020b). Taking Finnish basic education curriculum as an example, cultural diversity, differences in religious and non-religious worldviews, and intra-religious diversity might exert different influences on students' and children's development of spirituality (Ubani et al., 2020).

The rise of technology and use of virtual and media spaces as well as cyberspaces for communication, learning, gaming and work has induced new challenges and opportunities for probing into issues related to young people and children's spirituality. Some scholars such as Galik (2015) raise questions about whether "cyber-spirituality" might be a new form of religion (p. 5) or whether it would bring about characteristics such as "cyber-shamanism" or "techno-shamanism" (pp. 11, 13). Of course, we should try to minimize and avoid the phenomenon of cyber bullying which may have adverse impact on children's spirituality (Apostolides, 2017).

This edited volume focuses on different and complementary perspectives of children's spirituality in diverse and changing contexts. There is also a paper (Mata-McMahon, 2016) and an editorial (Lee, 2021) touch upon issues arising from a review of the published *IJCS* articles. Because of the limitations of the pages required by the publisher, there should be many more papers which could have been selected for inclusion. Readers are encouraged to follow up the website of the journal which has currently published volume 23 (2023) (www.tandfonline.com/toc/cijc20/current).

Acknowledgment

The authors would like to thank Ms Wendy Hoi Yi Liu for her assistance in preparing this chapter.

Disclosure statement

The views reflected in this article are personal views only and do not represent those of The Education University of Hong Kong and/or UNESCO and do not commit these respective organizations.

References

Adams, K. (2019). Navigating the spaces of children's spiritual experiences: Influences of tradition(s), multidisciplinarity and perceptions. *International Journal of Children's Spirituality*, 24(1), 29–43.

Adams, K., Bull, R., & Maynes, M-L. (2016). Early childhood spirituality in education: Towards an understanding of the distinctive features of young children's spirituality. *European Early Childhood Education Research Journal*, 24(5), 760–774.

Apostolides, A. (2017). Cyber bullying: Child and youth spirituality. *HTS Teologiese Studies/Theological Studies*, 73(3), a4692.

Champagne, E. (2008). Living and dying: A window on (Christian) children's spirituality. *International Journal of Children's Spirituality*, 13(3), 253–263.

Eaude, T. (2003). Shining lights in unexpected corners: New angles on young children's spiritual development. *International Journal of Children's Spirituality*, 8(2), 151–162.

Eaude, T. (2005). Strangely familiar? Teachers making sense of young children's spiritual development. *Early Years*, 25(3), 237–248.

Eaude, T. (2006). *Children's spiritual, moral, social and cultural development: Primary and early years*. Exeter: Learning Matters.

Eaude, T. (2018). Addressing the needs of the whole child: Implications for young children and adults who care for them. In J.P. Miller, K. Nigh, M.J. Binder, B. Novak and S. Crowell (Eds.), *International handbook of holistic education* (pp. 61–69). London: Routledge.

Editorial (1996). Spirituality and education. *International Journal of Children's Spirituality*, 1(1), 4–5.

Fisher, J. (2001). Comparing levels of spiritual well-being in state, catholic and independent schools in Victoria, Australia. *Journal of Beliefs and Values*, 22(1), 99–105.

Galik, S. (2015). Cyber-spirituality as a new form of religion. *European Journal of Science and Theology*, 11(6), 5–14.

Goodliff, G. (2013). Spirituality expressed in creative learning: Young children's imagining play as space for mediating their spirituality. *Early Child Development and Care*, 183(8), 1054–1071.

Harris, K. (2018). The personae of the spiritual child: Taking pictures of the heart using technology and tablets. *International Journal of Children's Spirituality*, 23(3), 291–305.

Hay, D. (1997). Spiritual education and values. *International Journal of Children's Spirituality*, 2(2), 5–16.

Hay, D. (1998, March). Why should we care about children's spirituality? *Pastoral Care*, 16(1), 11–16.

Hay, D. & Nye, R. (1996). Investigating children's spirituality: The need for a fruitful hypothesis. *International Journal of Children's Spirituality*, 1(1), 6–16. https://www.tandfonline.com/doi/abs/10.1080/1364436960010103

Hay, D. with Nye, R. (2006). *The spirit of the child* (rev. edn). London: Jessica Kingsley.

Hey, S. (2020). Spirituality for sustainable, inclusive, and equitable education. In W. Leal Filho, A.M. Azul, L. Brandli, P.G., Ozuyar & T. Wall (Eds.), *Quality education. Encyclopedia of the UN sustainable development goals* (pp. 802–811). Cham: Springer.

Lee, J.C.K. (2020a). Editorial: Children's spirituality, life and values education: Cultural, spiritual and educational perspectives. *International Journal of Children's Spirituality*, 25(1), 1–8.

Lee, J.C.K. (2020b). Editorial: Children's spirituality, life and religious education: Socio-cultural and religious traditions and perspectives. *International Journal of Children's Spirituality*, 25(2), 83–90.

Lee, J.C.K. (2021). Editorial: Children's spirituality: Personal reflections on International Journal of Children's Spirituality (IJCS). *International Journal of Children's Spirituality*, 26(1-2), 1–8, DOI: 10.1080/1364436X.2021.1879504

Mata-McMahon, J. (2016). Reviewing the research in children's spirituality (2005–2015): Proposing a pluricultural approach. *International Journal of Children's Spirituality*, 21(2), 140–152.

Ubani, M., Hyvarinen, E., Lemettinen, J., & Hirvonen, E. (2020). Dialogue, worldview inclusivity, and intra-religious diversity: Addressing diversity through religious education in the Finnish basic education curriculum. *Religions*, 11, 581.

Ubani, M. & Tirri, K. (2006). How do Finnish pre-adolescents perceive religion and spirituality? *International Journal of Children's Spirituality*, 11(3), 357–370.

Yust, K.-M., Hyde, B. & Ota, C. (2010). Editorial: Cyber spirituality: Facebook, Twitter, and the adolescent quest for connection. *International Journal of Children's Spirituality*, 15(4), 291–293.

Yust, K.-M., Hyde, B. & Ota, C. (2011). Editorial: Cyber spirituality II: Virtual reality and spiritual exploration. *International Journal of Children's Spirituality*, 16(1), 1–3.

Introduction—Children's spirituality: personal reflections on International Journal of Children's Spirituality (IJCS)

John Chi-Kin Lee

As quite many journals under major publishers such as Taylor and Francis are now running in both on-line and print versions, there may be interesting questions on the role of editorials. In a journal where I have been engaged as one of the executive editors, I remembered that in the past I could choose some accepted articles (already appeared online) to make a coherent theme and then write an editorial for an issue. It is quite an interesting but challenging task as it is not written as an editorial for a special issue of a journal. In addition, the journal papers are coming in, often revised and then accepted sporadically and sometimes unpredictably in terms of time and responses of authors, reviewers and editorial board members or associate editors especially the Editor and Book Review Editor who coordinates book reviews.

Rust (2018) quoted Purmalo and highlighted the importance of editorials to focus on issues that are crafted to 'provoke conversation rather than to represent a specific viewpoint' (p. 600). Moreover, she also indicated the function of honouring the scholarly contributions of these authors and the reviewers who spent time providing feedback and considering the papers as appropriate for publication in journals. Looking back to my first year of editorship of International Journal of Children's Spirituality (IJCS) in 2020, I would sincerely thank all old and new editorial board members, Dr Tony Eaude (Book Review Editor), Ms Abi Amey (Portfolio Manager), members of College of Reviewers and other reviewers for their hard work and valuable contributions.

In my past editorials, I have not quoted and cited the papers just accepted and published for an issue of IJCS partly because these papers altogether might not be very coherent in terms of concepts, themes or methodologies while individually they have made remarkable contributions and useful discourses to the literature of children's spirituality. It is also part of the reason that I would like to get acquainted to the 'protocols' of the IJCS's editorial system as well as the 'culture' of the editorial process. Under this backdrop, my editorials tend to refer to the works of some editorial board members as well as some of the possibly interesting educational issues related to children's spirituality as my academic background is more from curriculum and educational studies (Lee 2020a, 2020b).

In this editorial, I would like to take a snapshot of some of the figures of IJCS between 2009 and 2019 and offer some of my preliminary observations of the published papers in volume 25 (2020).

As shown in Table 1, it is expected that keywords such as spirituality, children and children's spirituality as well as spiritual well-being, well-being and spiritual development tend to be frequently used for indexing or highlighting the key themes or concepts in the published in IJCS or research on child spirituality (de Souza, Bone, and Watson 2016). In past published articles, there were terms such as children, youth and adolescents. According to The Convention on the Rights of the Child: The children's version (UNICEF 2019), 'A child is any person under the age of 18'. In addition, the children have the rights, among many others, to have 'life survival and development', 'freedom of thought and religion', 'sharing thoughts freely' and 'respect for children's views' by adults (UNICEF 2019). As regards the meaning of adolescence, it refers to transitional phase between childhood and adulthood (Csikszentmihalyi 2020) and adolescent is defined as any individual between ages 10 and 19 by World Health Organization (WHO). It is notable that 'youth' is defined as the age group between ages 15 and 24 and 'young people' as individuals having the age range 10–24 years, respectively, according to the World Health Organization (WHO) (Retrieved 3 January 2021 from https://www.who.int/southeastasia/health-topics/adolescent-health). For the IJCS, the scope of the journal covers children and young people and therefore for the age range, we might consider issues related to and/or pertinent to individuals probably any person below the age of 24 (Retrieved 3 January 2021 from https://www.tandfonline.com/action/journalInformation?show=aimsScope&journalCode=cijc20). Other more frequently cited keywords of the articles are related to education, religion, religiosity, God, religious education and spiritual education. Some articles have adopted other keywords such as relationship and identity. To a certain extent, these keywords frequently appeared in the abstracts echo the three categories of research on children's spirituality from 2005 to 2015 which encompass

Table 1. Frequency of keywords appeared in the International Journal of Children's Spirituality (IJCS) (2009–2019).

No.	Keywords	Count
1.	Spirituality	103
2.	Children	34
3.	Children's spirituality	18
4.	Education	12
5.	Religious education	12
6.	Adolescents	11
7.	Spiritual development	11
8.	Religion	10
9.	Spiritual well-being	10
10.	Well-being	8
11.	Youth	8
12.	Identity	7
13.	Spiritual education	7
14.	God	5
15.	Relationship	5
16.	Religiosity	5

spiritual meaning-making and relationships to/with God, children's spirituality in education as well as identity formation and sense of self (Mata-McMahon 2016, 140). From a developmental and spiritual perspective, there are a lot of changes when a child develops from infancy to adolescence. Surr (2014, 128), for example, pointed out that at the stage of early childhood, children might explore 'boundaries between reality, imagination and spirituality' while at the early adolescence, parents and adult mentors' support for children's wholeness is important (p. 129). Gellel (2018), for example, advocates and implements a symbolic literacy approach through interdisciplinary pedagogy for primary students in the Maltese context. Some scholars further emphasise the aspects of 'transcendence, fidelity, transformation and action' as well as elements of intentional living for adolescent spirituality (King and Boyatzis 2015; Gellel 2019, 124). Yust, Watson, and Hyde (2017, 107) further advise that if family support could not be adequately available for children's nurturance of spirituality at an early stage, educators, religious leaders and social service providers have to devote a lot of care and extra efforts in filling in the gap later. At the adolescence stage, programmes and framework with notions of 'cultivation of moral reasoning, ethical decision-making, virtuous character, and/or religious confirmation' are likely to be conducive to adolescent spirituality (Yust 2016, 81).

In Volume 25 (2020) of IJCS, a total of 15 papers contributed by scholars from different parts of world such as Australia, New Zealand, Thailand, Singapore, Iran, Belgium, Germany, the United Kingdom, South Africa and the United States were published excluding book reviews and editorials. It is not straightforward to cluster or group these papers as some of them could have some keywords or themes slightly overlapping in nature. Two papers, for example, have 'context' in their titles or sub-titles (Capitano and Naudé 2020; Dillen 2020) while another two papers touch upon the word 'context/contexts' in their abstracts (Hyde 2020, 197; Robinson 2020, 254).

It is noteworthy that some scholars such as Haugen (2018, 307) highlight the nature of nurturing children's spirituality being 'highly diverse, and context dependent' and spiritual development pertaining to 'meaning-making, enhanced awareness and connectedness'. Children's constructions of their identities are often shaped by culture and traditions (Eaude 2019, 1). A paper has a focus on the connections between relationships and context as well as the influences of parents, peers, the educational environment and geographical location in shaping South African adolescents' spirituality identity development (Capitano and Naudé 2020) while another paper highlights the context of a hospital or after a migration experience of children from a postcolonial theological perspective (Dillen 2020). Robinson's paper (2020, 254) discusses in Western Australia the early years' educators' perceptions and practices in promoting children's (3 and 4 years old) spirituality in faith-based early learning centres.

Spiritual formation and spiritual development of children and young people may hinge on their own identity development which may have different forms of expressions and various sources of influences (Ubani and Murtonen 2018, 103–104). Brailey and Parker (2020) paper examines the identity formation of Christian young adult from the perspective of Christian mentoring as a tool. de Kock (2020, 224) explores learning in encounter in Flanders (Belgium) and youth's spiritual development in Protestant evangelical faith communities. Hyde (2020, 197) provides a detailed account of using the evocative method of phenomenological inquiry and the anecdotes of adults as a powerful approach to unpacking children's expressions of spirituality under different contexts. Livingston (2020) instead explores youth athletes' and their parents' perceptions of the competitive environment as well as possible influence of church attendance on children's spirituality.

Three papers seem to be more related to spiritual care and spiritual needs of children with diseases or those with serious or chronic illness. Parkinson, Bray, and Kool's (2020) paper reveals that health professionals in New Zealand might have diverse views on the meaning and practices of spiritual care. Some of the findings suggest the importance of understanding child development and family's culture as well as the potentials of education and peer and self-reflection for enhancing the perspectives and practices of health professionals in spiritual care (Parkinson, Bray, and Kool 2020, pp. 64–65). In the paper by Thanattheerakul, Tangvoraphonkchai, and Pimsa (2020), the perceptions of spiritual needs and practice of chronically ill children and primary caregivers in the Isan region of Thailand are studied. The results reveal that their perceptions are to some extent related to the influence of Buddhism and Thai Isan traditions. The paper on the spiritual life and anxiety of children with immunodeficiency investigates the effect of prayer painting and the results tend to suggest prayer painting as a practice for reducing anxiety for these children (Zarei et al. 2020).

Some papers broadly pertain to materials and strategies for accessing and understanding children's religious concepts and spiritual formation. The study by Kaiser and Riegel (2020) indicates that boys and girls tend to use technical objects and natural motifs, respectively, to express their concepts of God which may be affected by gender-stereotypes. Another study on young people by Sewell (2020) using narrative approach and the theoretical perspective of theological aesthetics highlights the potentials of composite methods and visual strategies underpinned by diverse theoretical bases that could help unpack adolescent's spiritual narration and well-being. In a digital world where the use of technology is more prevalent, digital photographs taken by children followed by conversations could provide a powerful means for understanding children's spirituality (Harris 2018). The paper by Lucey and Lin (2020) discuss the introduction of critical compassion as an aspect of spirituality to the teaching and learning digital citizenship. More research could be conducted in the areas where technology might be employed to facilitate the children's spiritual development and cyber spirituality (Yust, Hyde, and Ota 2010).

In the literature of Christian writings, there is a concept of attentive presence for knowing God, self and others and nurturing integrated wholeness (Johnsen 2018, 53–54). The paper by Morris (2020) investigates the possible links between attentive presence and spiritual flourishing of children in the curatorial of worship through Participatory Action Research. In the East, Wu and Tan (2020) propose for preschool education a Neo-Confucian curriculum based on the notions of attentiveness and the writings of Zhu Xi around the concept of *jing* which is conducive to self-cultivation and the development of moral values. *Jing* proposed by Zhu Xi could be called single-minded and reverential attention (Tan 2019, 360–361) which is to some extent related to the reverence for interconnected life (Angle 2017). More dialogues could be engaged to discuss the implications of attentive presence, *jing*, other forms of reverential attention or mindfulness (Tan 2019) for life, religious and spiritual education.

Watson (2017, 12) asserts that in a post-secular spiritual landscape, spirituality connotes some key values such as spiritual diversity and inclusivity, every individual/child's human right to spiritual voice (because he/she still matters), an emphasis on the whole child (and person) and spiritual practice. Reading back and through these published papers with pleasure and respect, Volume 25 and other previous volumes of IJCS have provided us with a lot of diversified and enriched research findings as well as multi-disciplinary or interdisciplinary, thought-provoking ideas for further research and development in life, moral, religious and spiritual education for children and young people's spiritual development and spiritual well-being under diversified contexts.

Acknowledgments

The author would like to thank Dr Huang Jing, Mr Zhang Xingzhou and Ms Sharon Siu and Ms Hilton Cheung for their kind assistance in preparing this manuscript. The frequency of authors appeared in the *International Journal of Children's Spirituality* (IJCS) from 2009-2019 (including editorials) is checked and we would like to acknowledge the following authors/contributors with the frequency ranged from 5 to 32: Adrian Gellel, Ann M. Trousdale, Brendan Hyde, Cathy Ota, Jacqueline Watson, Jennifer Mata-McMahon, John Surr, Karen-Marie Yust, Kate Adams, Kathleen Harris, Marian de Souza, Ruth Wills, and Tony Eaude (in alphabetical order).

Disclosure statement

No potential conflict of interest was reported by the author.

Disclaimer

The views presented in this editorial are personal only and do not necessarily represent those of The United Nations Educational, Scientific and Cultural Organisation (UNESCO) and The Education University of Hong Kong, and do not commit the respective organisations.

References

Angle, S. C. 2017. "Zhu Xi's Breakthrough." *Harvard Divinity Bulletin*. Accessed 3 January 2021. https://bulletin.hds.harvard.edu/zhu-xis-breakthrough/

Brailey, G. S., and S. D. Parker. 2020. "The Identity Imperative: Mentoring as a Tool for Christian Young Adult Identity Formation." *International Journal of Children's Spirituality* 25 (2): 109–123. doi:10.1080/1364436X.2020.1819775.

Capitano, T. A., and L. Naudé. 2020. "Context as Co-creator in Spiritual Life Stories: The Contextual Nature of South African Adolescents' Spiritual Identity Development." *International Journal of Children's Spirituality* 25 (1): 9–29. doi:10.1080/1364436X.2020.1769567.

Csikszentmihalyi, M. 2020. "Adolescence." *Encyclopedia Britannica*. Accessed 3 January 2021. https://www.britannica.com/science/adolescence

de Kock, A. (Jos). 2020. "Learning in Encounter and Spiritual Development in Stressful Times: A Reflection from the Perspective of Protestant Evangelical Youth Ministry Practices in Flanders." *International Journal of Children's Spirituality* 25 (3–4): 224–237. doi:10.1080/1364436X.2020.1843008.

de Souza, M., J. Bone, and J. Watson, Eds. 2016. *Spirituality across Disciplines: Research and Practice*. The Netherlands: Springer. https://www.springer.com/gp/book/9783319313788

Dillen, A. 2020. "Children's Spirituality and Theologising with Children: The Role of 'Context'." *International Journal of Children's Spirituality* 25 (3–4): 238–253. doi:10.1080/1364436X.2020.1843412.

Eaude, T. 2019. "The Role of Culture and Traditions in How Young Children's Identities are Constructed." *International Journal of Children's Spirituality* 24 (1): 5–19. doi:10.1080/1364436X.2019.1619534.

Gellel, A.-M. 2018. "Towards a Symbol Literacy Approach in the Education of Children." *International Journal of Children's Spirituality* 23 (2): 109–121. doi:10.1080/1364436X.2018.1448761.

Gellel, A.-M. 2019. "Children and Spirituality." In *The Routledge International Handbook of Spirituality in Society and the Professions*, edited by L. Zsolnai and B. Flanagan, 120–126. London: Routledge.

Harris, K. 2018. "The Personae of the Spiritual Child: Taking Pictures of the Heart Using Technology and Tablets." *International Journal of Children's Spirituality* 23 (3): 291–305. doi:10.1080/1364436X.2018.1483324.

Haugen, H. M. 2018. "It Is a Time for a General Comment on Children's Spiritual Development." *International Journal of Children's Spirituality* 23 (3): 306–322. doi:10.1080/1364436X.2018.1487833.

Hyde, B. 2020. "Evoking the Spiritual through Phenomenology: Using the Written Anecdotes of Adults to Access Children's Expressions of Spirituality." *International Journal of Children's Spirituality* 25 (3–4): 197–211. doi:10.1080/1364436X.2020.1843006.

Johnsen, G. 2018. "The Attentive Leader: Living and Leading Fully Present to God, Self, and Others in a Distracted World." Unpublished project submitted to Doctor of Ministry

Committee in candidacy for the degree of Doctor of Ministry. Springfield, MO: Assemblies of God Theological Seminary. Accessed 3 January 2021. http://agts.edu/wp-content/uploads/2018/09/Johnsen_READER-APPROVED_12-11-17_LO-1.pdf

Kaiser, K., and U. Riegel. 2020. "Differences in Children's Concepts of God: A Replication Study Based on Creative Tasks with Different Materials." *International Journal of Children's Spirituality* 25 (3–4): 187–196. doi:10.1080/1364436X.2020.1826411.

King, P. E., and C. J. Boyatzis. 2015. "Religious and Spiritual Development." In *Handbook of Child Psychology and Developmental Science*, edited by M. E. Lamb, R. M. Lerner, and S. B. Bonner, 975–1021. Hoboken, NJ: John Wiley & Sons.

Lee, J. C. K. 2020a. "Children's Spirituality, Life and Values Education: Cultural, Spiritual and Educational Perspectives." *International Journal of Children's Spirituality* 25 (1): 1–8. doi:10.1080/1364436X.2020.1790774.

Lee, J. C. K. 2020b. "Children's Spirituality, Life and Religious Education: Socio-cultural and Religious Traditions and Perspectives." *International Journal of Children's Spirituality* 25 (2): 83–90. doi:10.1080/1364436X.2020.1832296.

Livingston, J. 2020. "Competitive Youth Athletes: Are They Choosing between God and Sports?" *International Journal of Children's Spirituality* 25 (1): 51–63. doi:10.1080/1364436X.2019.1708707.

Lucey, T. A., and M. Lin. 2020. "Ghosts in the Machine: Understanding Digital Citizenship as the Struggle of Students' Souls with Classroom Technology." *International Journal of Children's Spirituality* 25 (2): 91–108. doi:10.1080/1364436X.2020.1797641.

Mata-McMahon, J. 2016. "Reviewing the Research in Children's Spirituality (2005–2015): Proposing a Pluricultural Approach." *International Journal of Children's Spirituality* 21 (2): 140–152. doi:10.1080/1364436X.2016.1186611.

Morris, T. 2020. "Discovering Attentive Presence: Children as Agents for Spiritual Change in the Curatorial of Worship." *International Journal of Children's Spirituality* 25 (1): 30–50. doi:10.1080/1364436X.2019.1711025.

Parkinson, S., Y. Bray, and B. Kool. 2020. "How Do Health Professionals Provide Spiritual Care to Seriously Ill Children?" *International Journal of Children's Spirituality* 25 (1): 64–77. doi:10.1080/1364436X.2019.1701421.

Robinson, C. 2020. "To Be 'Formed' and 'Informed': Early Years' Educators' Perspectives of Spirituality and Its Affordance in Faith-based Early Learning Centres." *International Journal of Children's Spirituality* 25 (3–4): 254–271. doi:10.1080/1364436X.2020.1848810.

Rust, F. O. 2018. "Editorial: Are the Editorial Necessary?" *Teachers and Teaching: Theory and Practice* 24 (6): 599–603. doi:10.1080/13540602.2018.1477368.

Sewell, J. 2020. "Visual Strategies for Adolescent Spiritual Well-being." *International Journal of Children's Spirituality* 25 (2): 141–156. doi:10.1080/1364436X.2020.1823333.

Surr, J. 2014. "Children Growing Whole." *International Journal of Children's Spirituality* 19 (2): 123–132. doi:10.1080/1364436X.2014.924907.

Tan, C. 2019. "Rethinking the Concept of Mindfulness: A Neo-Confucian Approach." *Journal of Philosophy of Education* 53 (2): 359–373. doi:10.1111/1467-9752.12343.

Thanattheerakul, C., J. Tangvoraphonkchai, and W. Pimsa. 2020. "Spiritual Needs and Practice in Chronically Ill Children and Their Families in the Isan Region of Thailand." *International Journal of Children's Spirituality* 25 (2): 157–171. doi:10.1080/1364436X.2020.1827225.

Ubani, M., and S. Murtonen. 2018. "Issues in Spiritual Formation in Early Lifespan Contexts." *International Journal of Children's Spirituality* 23 (2): 103–108. doi:10.1080/1364436X.2018.1452557.

UNICEF. 2019. "The Convention on the Rights of the Child: The Children's Version." Accessed 3 January 2021. https://www.unicef.org/child-rights-convention/convention-text-childrens-version

Watson, J. 2017. "Every Child Still Matters: Interdisciplinary Approaches to the Spirituality of the Child." *International Journal of Children's Spirituality* 22 (1): 4–13. doi:10.1080/1364436X.2016.1234434.

Wu, S., and C. Tan. 2020. "Attentiveness for Children: Proposing a neo-Confucian Curriculum for Preschool Education." *International Journal of Children's Spirituality* 25 (2): 124–140. doi:10.1080/1364436X.2020.1821177.

Yust, K. M. 2016. "Adolescent Spirituality and Education." In *Spirituality across Disciplines: Research and Practice*, edited by M. de Souza, J. Bone, and J. Watson, 81–93. Cham, Switzerland: Cham.

Yust, K. M., B. Hyde, and C. Ota. 2010. "Cyber Spirituality: Facebook, Twitter, and the Adolescent Quest for Connection." *International Journal of Children's Spirituality* 15 (4): 291–293. doi:10.1080/1364436X.2010.539007.

Yust, K. M., J. Watson, and B. Hyde. 2017. "The Spiritual Challenges of the 'Cradle to Prison Pipeline'." *International Journal of Children's Spirituality* 22 (2): 107–109. doi:10.1080/1364436X.2017.1310401.

Zarei, N., A. S. Hoseini, N. I. Zadeh, and A. Kazemnejad. 2020. "The Effect of Prayer Painting on Spiritual Life and Anxiety in 7–11-year-old Children with Immunodeficiency." *International Journal of Children's Spirituality* 25 (3–4): 212–223. doi:10.1080/1364436X.2020.1843007.

Investigating children's spirituality: the need for a fruitful hypothesis

David Hay and Rebecca Nye

ABSTRACT
It is only recently that the spirituality of children as distinct from their religion has appeared as a subject of *academic* interest. This development permits us to investigate children's spirituality as an aspect of a more general category than that of religion. Spirituality is characterised here as a natural form of human awareness. Research evidence is offered to demonstrate that the 'natural' hypothesis is more resilient to scientific testing than other more reductionist interpretations of spirituality. The conceptual underpinning of a study of children's spirituality based on the hypothesis is described. The hypothesis appears to offer a fruitful way forward for research.

Spirituality as distinct from religion

Concern with the religious education of children has a formal history which can be traced back at least to Luther. It has of course a very much older informal history. In contrast, interest in children's spirituality as distinct from their religion is a new phenomenon. It began to emerge only gradually as a bi-product of the scientific study of religious experience towards the end of the Nineteenth Century (Hay, Nye & Murphy, 1996).

The most important figures *in* this development - G. Stanley Hall, E.D. Starbuck, James Leuba and pre-eminently William James - produced their major work in New England. Elsewhere (Hay, 1996a) one of us has hypothesised that it was the cultural importance of the conversion experience in that Puritan society, conjoined with late Nineteenth Century *angst* about the plausibility of religion, that led to scientific interest in the nature of conversion as a psychological phenomenon. The major legacy was James' theory of human spirituality, announced in the twentieth of his Gifford Lectures at Edinburgh University in 1902 (published in the same year as *The Varieties of Religious Experience*). James, as a child of both New England· Puritan religion and the European Enlightenment, attempted to identify a religious or spiritual universal in the human species, not confined by any specific social constructions or, as he referred to them, 'over-beliefs'. Our equivocation between 'religious' and 'spiritual' is significant. It represents a continuing blurred boundary between the two terms, because many of the leading investigators in this field, including James, have failed to make a clear distinction between them. Our intention is to consider 'spiritual experience' as a term which includes but is broader than 'religious experience'. James' hypothesis was,

> ...... that whatever it may be on its *farther* side, the 'more' with which in religious experience we feel ourselves connected is on its *hither* side the subconscious continuation of our conscious life. Starting thus with a recognized psychological fact as our basis, we seem to preserve a contact with 'science' which the ordinary theologian lacks.......... Disregarding the over-beliefs, and confining ourselves to what is common and generic, we have in *the fact that the* conscious *person is continuous with a wider self through which saving experience come,* a positive content of religious experience which it seems to me, *is literally and objectively true as far as it goes.* (James, 1985, pp. 403, 405).

Later in the same lecture, James goes on to say that as part of his own Christian over-belief 'God' is the natural appellation for the supreme reality encountered in our religious experience. At this point he is making a distinction between the 'sign' and the 'signified' which since the lectures of Ferdinand de Saussure (Saussure, 1960) has been a commonplace of scholarly discussion. The distinction enabled him to postulate in the abstract a realm of awareness located in the makeup of the human species which is in a dialectical relationship with the language and traditions of a multitude of cultures.

It is important to add that it is through language, and only through language that, in innumerable forms, the postulated spirituality can emerge into the public domain. Nevertheless whilst remaining aware of this constraint the possibility emerges of using the notion of 'spirituality in general' as a research tool, rather than confining ourselves to Christian, Muslim, Buddhist or any other historically identifiable spiritualities. Whilst controversial (cf. the critiques of Katz, 1978; and Lindbeck, 1984) the perspective is not novel. Apart from William James there is a long line of European scholarly thought which implicitly requires a similar assumption, beginning with Schleiermacher (1799) and subsequently exemplified in the work of Ernst Troeltsch (1906), Rudolph Otto (1917), Joachim Wach (1958), Mircea Eliade (1960) and Alister Hardy (1966, 1979).

There is heuristic value in the idea of a natural spirituality. We could for example consider whether it might be reasonable to speak of spirituality in children without formal connection to any religious institution. It is this possibility which has in very recent years generated an interest in investigating the experience of children whose construction of reality is proceeding where the language and thought forms of traditional religion are marginalised or have lost their plausibility. If spirituality has a natural basis then we could expect children to show it in behaviour and language, even without teaching or religious exposure. But where we search depends on what parameters we give to the term spirituality.

An holistic understanding of spirituality

Like all interesting words, 'spirituality' defies simple definition and is best understood from an examination of the way it is used. At one end of the scale we speak of certain people as having a spiritual nature, with the connotation that they have a delicacy of awareness in relation to their surroundings. They may for example demonstrate a musical or poetic sensitivity. In this case there is no assumption that they will have any formal or even informal religious commitment. At the other extreme, the spiritual adept is someone who in mystical experience has discovered their oneness with the rest of reality or, if they are religiously devout, they aspire to or have achieved mystical union with the Godhead.

In spite of the extreme divergence, there is a degree of common ground between the ends of this continuum, for both refer to heightened awareness or attentiveness. We conjecture that spirituality in general is concerned with an awareness of and reflection upon the self and an holistic awareness of all that is not the self. This includes the paradoxical possibility, asserted in the Buddhist doctrine of *anatta*, that there is no 'self of which to be aware. Raised awareness itself constitutes spirituality, as indeed is taught in Buddhist *vipassana* meditation. But this is not a peculiarity of Buddhism. It is implied in all forms of religious meditation, including Christian contemplative prayer where one places oneself in the presence of God.

The *crucial* shift made in this holistic interpretation of spirituality is that it partially transcends the agenda of much modern debate about religious education. Spirituality is not in the first place about knowledge, though it is about a 'knowing' that becomes the subject of the processes of cognitive development. To that extent, the cognitive bias of contemporary theories of religious development (cf. Goldman, 1964; Fowler, 1981; Fowler, Nipkow & Schweitzer, 1991; Oser & Reich, 1990; Oser & Scarlett, 1991) has relevance to what is being considered here. But they fail to consider directly the implications of interpreting spirituality as a natural dimension of human awareness. To ignore this is potentially to leave spirituality as a somewhat fragile social construction and, as such, dangerously unanchored and open to the relativising wilderness of postmodernism.

The biological[1] hypothesis

After a period of stagnation in the 1930s, engendered by the twin influences of behaviorism and early (but not later) psychoanalysis (Beit-Hallahmi, 1974; Hay 1996a), the scientific study of spirituality reemerged in the 1960s, particularly through the work of the Oxford zoologist Alister Hardy (Hardy, 1966; 1979). In his Gifford Lectures given at Aberdeen University in 1965, he proposed a biological interpretation of 'religious experience' by which he meant spiritual awareness that is important enough to influence a person's life significantly. He drew particularly on William James' Gifford lectures and on the empirical work of James' student E.D.Starbuck (1901) on experiences of Puritan conversion in the New England of his own day. Hardy's contribution to the development of the ideas of James and Starbuck was to emphasise the biological basis of spirituality. He suggested that spiritual awareness had evolved through natural selection during the process of evolution because of its survival value to the individual. If he is right, the potential to encounter spiritual experience and awareness may be available to every normal child.

Hardy's hypothesis is of more than scientific interest. Although it is naturalistic it differs from other contemporary scientific conjectures about spirituality, in that Hardy did not intend to be reductionist. He saw spiritual awareness as something entirely positive and necessary for human survival. Furthermore, because his hypothesis is

---

[1] Some confusion may be caused by the use *of* the word 'biological'. Psychologists tend to apply the term rather narrowly to mean the strictly anatomical side of psychology, as in neuro-anatomy. Biologists use the word in a broader sense to refer to any natural properties of living organisms. It is in this latter way that we wish to be understood.

naturalistic, it is potentially possible to examine its relative resilience under scientific testing in comparison with other postulates. At the time of writing, Hardy's idea stands up well in comparison to other more prominent reductionist conjectures, including Marx's (1844) 'opium of the people' hypothesis, Freud's (1928) assumption that 'religious experience' is symptomatic of neurosis, and Durkheim's association of spiritual experience with social 'effervescence'. The data are discussed in detail in Hay (1994). Briefly, the findings are as follows:

Spiritual experience is widely reported in Britain. Questions placed in a Gallup Omnibus Survey in Britain in 1986 revealed that about half those surveyed felt they had had such experience (Hay & Heald, 1987). A series of in-depth studies on particular sub-populations in England (Hay, 1979; Hay & Morisy, 1985; Lewis, 1985) where there is time to build up rapport with those being interviewed suggests the probability that about two-thirds of the adult population are aware of a spiritual dimension to their experience.

Contrary to what could be predicted from Marx's postulate, at least in Britain, people who might be classed as 'oppressed' (the inner city poor; the long term unemployed) are less likely than others to speak of spirituality. In part this may be due to inarticulacy because of an underprivileged education, but it could also be seen simply as a further dimension of the psychological damage created by unjust social conditions.

There is a statistically significant association between report of experience and good education, personal happiness and good mental health as assessed by the Bradburn Balanced Affect Scale (Bradburn. 1969). This suggests that. at the least, we need to be wary of Freud's dismissal of religious experience (and hence spirituality in the sense we have been using the term) as symptomatic of neurosis.

Finally, most people say that their spiritual awareness is at its greatest when they are alone. This sharply contradicts Durkheim's 'social effervescence' hypothesis, which suggests that religious experience 'is' the excitement experienced by people involved in large and excited religious gatherings.

In crude terms then, these hypotheses do not stand up well against Hardy's conjecture. But a prudent caution is in order. In coming to consider the ideas of these past masters as we reach the end of the 20th century we are always in danger of 'conceptual slippage'. Marx, Freud and Durkheim were writing specifically about religion, using the intellectual frameworks available to them in their time. It is not clear that they would be as intolerant of spirituality in the wider sense to which we refer. This is an added complexity which we have to acknowledge.

Nevertheless, we believe the findings referred to increase the plausibility of Hardy's hypothesis and also imply certain expectations about children's spirituality. If the suggestion is correct, one might suppose that in a secularised culture spirituality would be more prominent in childhood than in adult life. It could be conjectured that this is because the socially constructed pattern of modern Western cultural assumptions has created an overlay which obscures the natural spirituality of the human species. There is both anecdotal and scientific evidence providing at least tentative support for such a view. Writing in the 19th century at a point when post-Enlightenment scepticism was allied with the accelerating social effects of the Industrial Revolution, William Wordsworth was in no doubt that the transcendent insights of childhood become clouded in adult life. Elsewhere (Hay, Nye & Murphy, 1996) we have reviewed the evidence for the continuance of the same process in the 20th century. Most prominent is the work of Kalevi Tamminen in Finland (Tamminen, 1991). who questioned over 3000 children and young people about what he calls their 'personal religious experience' and showed that whilst it is commonly spoken of in childhood, from the age of about twelve or thirteen years it becomes Jess and Jess frequently reported.

Identifying spirituality in a secular culture

We have been working with children aged six and ten years in Nottingham and Birmingham and have had to consider how spirituality might be given expression at the fringes of its traditional vehicle in European culture, the language of Christian theology. Here we are sharing the difficulties of others who have embarked on somewhat parallel research (cf. Erricker & Erricker, 1994; Erricker, Sullivan, Erricker, Logan & Ota, 1994; McCreery, 1994). Where the language and institutions of formal religion are absent or unconvincing for many people. we had to try to identify the areas of children's language and behaviour where the 'sparks of spirituality' may be found.

For this purpose we needed to create a hypothetical map as a kind of template to guide our conversations with children. We examined the converging evidence of writers on spirituality and on child psychology, as well as our own experience of talking with children in the pilot stage of the project. As a result we proposed a set of three inter-related themes or categories of spiritual sensitivity

> (Nye & Hay, 1996) which were basic enough to allow expression within or outside the familiar (usually religious) languages of spirituality. The intention is to make possible the identification of spirituality in a wider and more abstract context than has been achieved elsewhere. We will thus be able to move beyond an understanding of children's· spirituality based on 'knowledge' towards a more general psychological domain of spirituality as a basic form of knowing, available to us *all* as part of our biological inheritance.

A TABLE OF CATEGORIES OF SPIRITUAL SENSITIVITY

AWARENESS SENSING	Here and Now
	Tuning
	Flow
	Focusing
MYSTERY SENSING	Awe and Wonder
	Imagination
VALUE SENSING	Delight and Despair
	Ultimate Goodness
	Relationship
	Meaning

(Adapted from Nye & Hay, 1996)

These categories are discussed at length in the paper referred to above. In summary, the themes we identified as likely to be present within childhood spirituality were as follows:

Awareness Sensing: Or, being aware of one's awareness. In particular this can mean an awareness of the *here and now,* instead of letting the mind wander into the past and future, something which characterises much of adult life. Margaret Donaldson (1992) calls this the 'point mode', the most basic mode of the mind's operation and, as such, present in even the youngest child. Religious interest in the point mode spreads across all cultures and expresses itself in the practice of meditation and contemplative prayer. This of course does not mean that all of children's early experience is in some way recognised as spiritual. Being aware of one's awareness is what creates the spiritual significance, and it may be that at first this only emerges retrospectively in contrast to other modes of mental operation.

Eugene Gendlin (1962) talks of total bodily awareness of the here-and-now as *focusing* on what he calls the 'felt sense' of a situation. It implies a recovery of respect for the body as a source of spiritual knowledge and is the natural mode of knowing in young children before they become inducted into the dominant cognitive tradition of Western culture. The 'felt sense' has a direct bearing on many forms of religious meditation (Campbell & McMahon, 1985).

Another way of considering heightened awareness is through Alfred Schutz's (1964) metaphor of *tuning*. Tuning for Schutz is the kind of awareness which can arise in aesthetic experience, for example when listening to music. Feeling 'at one' with nature, which is a commonly reported context for adult recollection of childhood spiritual experience, might be an illustration of this type of awareness.

Csikszentmihalyi (1975) looks particularly at the experience of *flow*. This refers to the liberating sense of one's activity managing itself, or being managed by some outside influence, so that a task which previously seemed complex and demanding transforms into a single flow. It has been suggested that the spiritual exercises of St Ignatius are a formal attempt to generate flow (Csikszentmihalyi, 1988). For the child who is almost daily mastering new skills, the experience of flow is potentially very familiar, given the ability to reflect upon or become self conscious of this awareness.

Mystery-Sensing: Mystery here refers to our experience of realities that are *in principle* incomprehensible. Rudolf Otto (1950) identifies two sides to our experience of mystery, fascination or *wonder,* and fear or awe. Awareness of things beyond one's current understanding is very familiar in childhood and here it is important to make a clear discrimination. For the older child, the explanations provided by education often created a 'scientific' superstition which implies that there are answers to everything, and displaces or even represses the true mysteriousness of existence. It is important that in the process of education a recognition of mystery is matured rather than dismissed as infantile thinking.

Mundane experience is transcended through imagery and metaphor in the deployment of *imagination*. Probing mystery requires the imagination to conceive what is beyond the known and what is 'obvious'. Studies of children's ability to enter into fantasy show they have a powerful capacity for (and enjoyment of) letting go of material reality, or using it in a new way to discover meanings and values in response to their experience, especially experience for which their language is inadequate (Hammond, Hay et al., 1990). Imagination is of course central to religious activity through the metaphors, symbols, stories and liturgies which respond to the otherwise unrepresentable experience of the sacred. The fact that these responses are all cultural products demonstrates the importance of the interplay between nature and nurture. Our hypothesis is fundamentally about this interaction, whilst at the same time insisting on taking seriously the natural pole of the relationship.

Value-Sensing: The term 'value-sensing' in relation to feeling was coined by Margaret Donaldson (1992). She states that the degree of affect is a measure of value, reflecting a stance towards what is felt to matter. It is because the matter of spirituality is of central existential importance that it is associated with strong feeling. Indeed the emotions associated with such value-sensing are commonly reported as profound. Hence we have adopted the terms *delight* and *despair*.in reference to them, intending to convey something of the intensity of the emotions associated with spiritual awareness. It is a commonplace of our experience of children that they are, at least if their upbringing is adequate, easily in touch with the intense awareness that generates delight or despair.

Peter Berger (1970) proposes that the sense of ultimate goodness is transmitted to children from the earliest age through the comforting language of parents, conveying a sense of ultimate order and pattern in the face of the child's fear of chaos and disharmony. It could be suggested that awareness of this is a prerequisite for being able to entertain the intuition of the goodness of God. That is to say, the absence of a context of security in childhood nurture makes it difficult or impossible to conceive of such security at the cosmic level. We are thinking here of the work of Godin and others who have considered the role of projection in the creation of images of God (cf. Godin & Hallez, 1965; Deconchy, 1968; Spilka, Addison & Rosensohn, 1975).

Earlier we mentioned our expectation that we would discover further categories of experience related to spirituality as the research progressed. It is here that we wish to insert the category of *relationship* which has surfaced repeatedly in conversations with children as a sensitivity or awareness characteristic of the spiritual. Though we overlooked it originally, its appearance is hardly surprising since our general characterisation of spirituality is that it is about our relationship both with the s·elf and holistically with all that is not ourselves. It is here in particular that the intensity of feeling emerges which Donaldson characterises as an indicator of value. Religious ideas that spring to mind as being linked with this include Martin Suber's emphasis on 'I *and* Thou' (Suber, 1970) and John Cumpsty's more recent theory of religion as 'belonging' (Cumpsty, 1991). We take it that our initial blindness to this major dimension of spirituality arises at least in part from our socialisation within a highly individualistic culture. We are tempted to *the* suggestion that the polar opposite of 'spirituality' is 'individualism'.

Meaning is our final subcategory. This has been a guiding category for several researchers into the nature of religion from a predominantly cognitive perspective, including James Fowler (1981) on faith as a meaningful personal framework, and Daniel Batson's (Batson, Schoenrade & Ventis, 1993) emphasis on the spiritual quest as a search for ultimate meaning. 'Meaning' is certainly of central importance in relation to children's spirituality. At the same time we criticise the proponents of a purely cognitive approach for their tendency to ignore the existential basis for the creation of religious meaning. Questions of meaning which are essentially spiritual are raised by young children: Who am I? Where do I belong? What is my purpose? To whom or what am I connected or responsible? We suggest that these more cognitive signs of spiritual activity are in many cases the secondary products of spiritual stirrings found in awareness-, mystery- and value-sensing.

Setting an agenda

In textbooks of scientific methodology it is usual to find reference to the importance of the 'fruitfulness' of an hypothesis. Fruitfulness implies that in the process of testing the conjecture numerous rich new ideas are generated, producing a deeper understanding of the phenomenon being examined. Sometimes it is even suggested that a fruitful though mistaken hypothesis is to be preferred to a correct hypothesis which propagates few ideas.

Time will tell whether Hardy's hypothesis about the nature of human spirituality continues to behave resiliently under scientific scrutiny. It is already clear that it is capable of creating new and potentially fertile ways of considering children's spirituality. By locating spirituality in the human organism it places a focus on childhood and on spirituality as intrinsic rather than taught. As a conclusion to this paper we offer three examples of major ways forward for research, that are implied by the biological hypothesis. Whilst these research perspectives are independent at the conceptual level, they are tightly inter-related in reality.

1. *Children's spirituality and metaphor.* The utility of postmodernism (taken in small doses) is that it breaks up all dogmatisms, secular as well as religious. It releases us from the tyranny of what William Blake called 'single vision'. Significantly, Blake had Isaac Newton particularly in mind when he used that phrase. The single vision of 'scientism' (the superstitious idea that science can solve all problems and, unlike other human endeavours, is somehow independent of the fallible human beings who engage in it) certainly seems to play a part in the suppression of spirituality in some ten-year-old children.

   Nevertheless, from a critical realist perspective a belief in a stable reality which is apprehended in multiform ways through humanly created metaphor, is not excluded by this loosening up. There are important questions to be asked about the precise role of metaphor in mediating this reality to us (cf. Erricker, Sullivan, Erricker, Logan & Ota, 1994; Hay, Nye & Murphy, 1996; Nye & Hay, 1996; McCreery, 1996). Could we for example construct an argument round the notion that metaphor opens up or obscures our experience of the spiritual dimension of our awareness? How adequate in mediating spirituality are the dominant metaphor systems to which modern children are introduced either formally in the classroom or informally at home or via the media? What seems to be called for is a much deeper investigation of the function of metaphor, perhaps guided by the insights of hermeneuticists like Paul Ricoeur.

2. *Spiritual education and social cohesion.* One of the most important research findings about spiritual experience is its association with ethics (Hay, 1996b). Almost without exception adults questioned about the influence of their spiritual insight say that it motivates an increased desire to care for those closest to them, to take issues of social justice more seriously and to be concerned about the total environment. The source of these outcomes is the recognition that the 'psychological distance' between oneself and the rest of reality is illusory. This is experienced either in the form of an intuition that damage to any part of the fabric of reality is damage to oneself, or in religious mode, as a realization that the love of God implies care for the whole of his creation. These findings have a

central bearing on the creation of social cohesion. To quote Philip Selznick (1992) the question is, how can we promote the establishment of a 'Moral Commonwealth' to replace the extreme alienation, even criminality, with which much of our society is plagued? It has become clear from recent history, that external motivations do not work very well, whether through exhortation, threat, training programmes or short sharp shocks. The importance of the built-in spirituality of the individual is that it is intrinsic. Spirituality cannot be taught. It can be and is very often crushed out of awareness during education. We urgently need to understand more about the processes that produce spiritual damage, so that they can be countered adequately, particularly in the school classroom.

3. *How do nature and nurture interact in the development of children's spirituality?* Here we need to take account of recent attempts to bridge a sometimes acrimonious gulf. A landmark in this difficult area was the publication of William Durham's magisterial book *Co-Evolution: Genes, Culture and Human Diversity* (Durham, 1991). Durham suggests that cultural selection parallels natural selection in important ways and goes on to consider how biological-cultural factors interact in particular settings. One of his important suggestions is that cultural change can be at odds with the requirements of biology, creating pathological consequences. Could the treatment of spirituality in contemporary Western culture be an illustration, particularly in the way it is handled with children?

References

Batson, D., Schoenrade, P. & Ventis, L.W. (1993). *Religion and the Individual: A social psychological perspective*. New York: Oxford University Press.

Beit-Hallahmi, B. (1974). 'Psychology of religion 1880–1930: the rise and fall of a psychological movement'. *Journal of the History of the Behavioral Sciences*. 10, 84.

Berger, P. (1970). *A Rumor of Angels*. London: Allen Lane/Penguin Press. Bradburn, N. (1969). *The Structure of Psychological Wellbeing*. Chicago: Aldine Press.

Buber, M. (1970). *I and Thou* (W.Kaufmann trans.) New York: Scribners.

Campbell, P. & McMahon, E. (1985). *Biospirituality: Focusing as a Way to Grow*. Chicago: Loyola University Press.

Csikszentmihalyi, I. (1988). 'Flow in a historical context: the case of the Jesuits' in, Mihaly Csikszentmihalyi & Isabella Csikszentmihalyi (eds.), *Psychological Studies of Flow in Consciousness*, New York: Cambridge University Press, pp. 232–248. Csikszentmihalyi, M. (1975). *Beyond Boredom and Anxiety*, San Francisco: Jessey Bass.

Cumpsty, J. (1991). *Religion as Belonging: A General Theory of Religion*. London: University Press of America.

Deconchy, J.P. (1968). 'God and parental images', in A. Godin (Ed.) *From Cry to Word*, Brussels: Lumen Vitae Press, pp. 85–94.

Donaldson, M. {1992). *Human Minds*, London: Allen Lane/Penguin Press.

Durham, W. (1991). *Coevolution: Genes, Culture and Human Diversity*. Stanford University Press.

Durkheim, E. (1915). *The Elementary Forms of the Religious Life*, (tr. J.W. Swain), London: George Allen & Unwin.

Eliade, M. (1960). *Myths, Dreams and Mysteries*, London: Harvill Press.

Erricker, C. & Erricker, J. (1994). 'Where angels fear to tread: discovering children's spirituality'. Paper presented at the Roehampton Conference, Education, Spirituality and the Whole Child, July 15–16.

Erricker, C., Sullivan, D., Erricker, J., Logan, J. & Ota, C. (1994). 'The development of children's worldviews', *Journal of Beliefs and Values*, 15(2), 3–6.

Fowler, J.W. (1981). *Stages of Faith*. New York: Harper & Row.

Fowler, J.W., Nipkow, K.E. & Schweitzer, F. (eds.) (1991). *Stages of Faith and Religious Development: Implications for Church, Education and Society*. London: SCM Press.
Freud, S. (1928). *The Future of an Illusion*. London: Hogarth Press.
Gendlin, E. (1962). *Experiencing and the Creation of Meaning*. Glencoe: Free Press.
Godin, A. & Hallez, M. (1965). 'Parental images and divine paternity', in A. Godin (Ed.). *From Religious Experience to Religious Attitude*, Chicago: Loyola University Press, pp. 65–96
Goldman, R. (1964). *Religious Thinking from Childhood to Adolescence*. London: Routledge & Kegan Paul.
Hammond, J., Hay, D. Moxon, J., Netto, B., Raban, K.. Straugheir, G., & Williams, C. (1990). *New Methods in RE Teaching: An Experiential Approach*, London: Oliver & Boyd/Longmans.
Hardy, A. (1966). *The Divine Flame*. London: Collins.
Hardy, A. (1979). The Spiritual Nature of Man. Oxford: Clarendon Press. Hay, D. (1994). '"The biology of God": What is the current status of Hardy's hypothesis?', *International Journal for the Psychology of Religion*, 4(1). 1–23.
Hay, D. (1996a) 'Interpreting conversion: the role of psychology in the rise of the hermeneutics of suspicion in the United States' (Unpublished paper).
Hay, D. (1996b). 'The politics of spiritual education'. Paper presented at the SCAA Symposium on Moral and Spiritual Education, Queen Elizabeth Conference Centre, London. Jan. 15.
Hay, D. & Heald, G. (1987). 'Religion is good for you'. *New Society*. April 17.
Hay, D. & Morisy, A. (1985). 'Secular society/religious meanings: a contemporary paradox'. *Review of Religious Research*. 26(3), 213.
Hay, D., Nye, R. & Murphy, R. (1996) Thinking about Childhood Spirituality: A Review of Research and Some Current Directions', in Leslie J. Francis, William K. Kay & William Campbell (eds.) *Research in Religious Education*, Leominster: Gracewing Press.
James, W. (1985). *The Varieties of Religious Experience*, Harvard University Press (originally published 1902).
Katz. S. (ed.) (1978). *Mysticism and Philosophical Analysis*. New York: Oxford University Press.
Lewis, D. (1985). 'All in good faith'. *Nursing Times*, March 18/24, 40.
Lindbeck, G. (1984). *The Nature of Doctrine: Religion and Theology in a Postlibera/ Age*, Philadelphia: The Westminster Press.
McCreery, E. (1994). 'Talking to young children about things spiritual'. Paper presented at the Roehampton Conference, Education, Spirituality and the Whole Child, July 15–16.
Marx, K. (1844). 'Introduction to the critique of Hegel's philosophy of right' *Deutsche-Franzosische Jahrbucher, 1844* (Reprinted in, K. Marx & F. Engels *On Religion*, Moscow: Progress Publishers, 1957).
Nye, R. & Hay, D. (1996). 'Identifying children's spirituality: how do you start without a starting point'. *British Journal of Religious Education* 18 (3), 144–154.
Oser, F. & Reich, K.H. (1990). 'Moral judgment, religious judgment, world views and logical thought: a review of their relationship'. *British Journal of Religious Education*, 12, 94–101, 172–181.
Oser, F. & Scarlett, W.G. (eds.) (1991) *Religious Development in Childhood and Adolescence*, San Francisco: Jossey-Bass.
Otto, R. (1950}. *The Idea of the Holy*. Oxford University Press (Originally published in German in 1917)
Saussure. F. de (1960) *Course in General Linguistics*. London: Peter Owen.
Schleiermacher, F. (1958). *On Religion: Speeches to its Cultured Despisers* (tr. John Oman) New York: Harper Torchbooks (Original German Edition, 1799).
Schutz. A. (1964). 'Making music together: a study in social relationship' in Arvid Brodersen (ed.), *Collected Papers II: Studies in Social Theory*. The Hague: Martinus Nijhoff, 135–158.
Selznick, P. (1992). *The Moral Commonwealth*. Berkeley: University of California Press.
Spilka, B., Addison, J. & Rosensohn, M. (1975). 'Parents, self and God: a test of competing theories of individual-religion relationships, *Review of Religious Research*, 6, 28–36.
Starbuck, E.D. (1901). *The Psychology of Religion*. New York: Walter Scott.
Tamminen, K. (1991). *Religious Development in Childhood and Youth: An Empirical Study*, Helsinki: Suomalainen Tiedeakatemia.
Troeltsch, E. (1906), 'Das Wesen der Religion und der Religionsgeschichte', (tr. Robert Morgan & Michael-Pye) in, *Ernst Troe/tsch: Writings on Theology and Religion*, Atlanta: John Knox Free Press, 1977.
Wach, J. (1958). *The Comparative Study of Religions*, New York: Columbia University Press.

Reviewing the research in children's spirituality (2005–2015): proposing a pluricultural approach

Jennifer Mata-McMahon

ABSTRACT
Research on children's spirituality seems to continue to be scarcely represented in the field of early childhood. In reviewing the literature, looking at empirical data-driven studies, this paper compiles an international review of the work completed in the last 10 years (2005–2015) on the topic of children's spirituality. The research-based works reviewed are analysed and sorted taking into account: research methods, participant demographics (age, gender, ethnicity) and location (urban vs. suburban/rural, school vs. home), yet are presented in categories found related to their topic of study: (1) spiritual meaning-making and relationships to/with God, (2) children's spirituality in education and (3) identity formation and sense of self. Finally, identification of gaps in the research literature regarding the study of children's spirituality is presented. As well, avenues for future research are proposed, identifying methods and approaches. Also, the term *pluricultural* as a means to guide researchers in making sense of the complex phenomenon that is children's spirituality is introduced.

Introduction and purpose

In spite of the importance of the topic, research on children's spirituality continues to be scarcely represented in the field of early childhood. Nevertheless, there have been some interesting empirical research studies looking into matters of spirituality and relating these to children. These studies' findings continue to forge advancement in the field. The purpose of this paper is to present in an organised fashion, the empirical studies completed in the last 10 years (2005–2015), looking into different aspects of and avenues for children's spirituality.

In order to achieve the proposed purpose, it is imperative that some parameters be made in regard to what will be reviewed. First, regarding the age of the children participating in the studies reviewed, the emphasis will be made on studies looking at children from birth to age nine, which generally is understood as the early childhood years. Yet, since there seems to be a scarcity of empirical research conducted with young children, the age span will be broadened to also include the early teenage years.

Second, since the primary focus is placed on empirical research conducted to explore and explain children's spiritual concepts and experiences, empirical studies and not theoretical ones, that make use of social science research methods and analysis (Ratcliff 2010), will be the type of research reviewed. Since spirituality is such an ethereal concept, difficult to define and measure, most empirical studies reviewed concentrate around the analysis of qualitative data, with an in-depth look at smaller numbers of participants, with no intent of generalisation of findings. It is important to also note, that this review intends to look at a specific selection of relevant research published in this topic, and does not claim to be exhaustive.

Third, regarding the definition of spirituality, studies defining spirituality as non-religious will be taken into account, as well as those studies that use religious spirituality as their framework. It is never an easy task to achieve consensus with what is meant by spirituality, since 'it is the nature of spirituality to be elusive' (Taggart 2001, 323). Nevertheless, for the purpose of clarity, definitions of both non-religious and religious spirituality will be offered, before beginning the review of the research.

In the edited volume on the topic of nurturing children's spirituality, Allen (2008) presents a review of different definitions of spirituality. Even though there are many definitions of non-religious spirituality, Allen (2008) explains that two common themes seem to be found in these various descriptions: 'self-transcendence and relationality – that is, relationship with self, others, the world, and perhaps with the transcendent' (7). To exemplify this, Lewis (2000) succinctly defines non-religious spirituality as 'an orientation towards ourselves and our relations with all other things' (274). Similarly, de Souza (2004) beautifully explains it as a movement towards the Ultimate Unity, 'whereby at the deepest and widest levels of connectedness, an individual may experience unity with the Other (Austin 2000; Newberg et al. 2001)' (Hyde 2008b, 118).

Regarding the definition of religious spirituality, of the many descriptions available, Allen (2008) presents religious spirituality as

> the intrinsic human capacity for self-transcendence in which the individual participates in the sacred ... [spirituality] is experienced, formed, shaped, and expressed through a wide range of religious narratives, beliefs, and practices, and is shaped by many influences in family, community, society, culture, and nature. (Yust et al. 2006, 7, 8)

Stemming from Allen (2008) and Lewis (2000) compilation of definitions, the two definitions presented above will be the working definitions for non-religious and religious spirituality anchoring this review of the research.

Methodology

In order to complete the review of the research published, a search was conducted using the following search terms: Child* Spirit*, Child* Religio*, Youth Spirit*, Youth Religio*. These terms were then combined with the following terms, to ensure the search would reach international contexts: international, global, United Kingdom, Australia, New Zealand, Asia, Latin America, Canada, Europe, Global South. The databases through which the search was conducted were: ERIC, Educational Research Complete, Health Source: Nursing/Academic Edition, Humanities Abstracts (H.W. Wilson), JSTOR, PsycINFO, Social Science Abstracts (H.W. Wilson) and Women's Studies International. And finally, the peer-reviewed journal on which the search mainly focused, because of its pertinence to the topic investigated, was the International Journal of Children's Spirituality.

Selecting this particular journal and the works there published is not to say that children's spirituality is not being considered in other fields, namely: health, counselling, and positive psychology, represented in other salient academic journals. Andrews and Marotta's (2005) qualitative phenomenological study on the role spirituality plays for grieving children, and how meaning-making and relationships help them cope with loss, is an excellent example of a study from the field of counselling that would inform this paper, if I had set to explore all fields with studies on children's spirituality. Yet, coming from an early childhood education background, my interest in the topic of children's spirituality is viewed through the lens of teaching and learning, and is deeply rooted in a constructivist and progressive educational perspective (Dewey 1938). Thus, the search for research on this topic was completed through the lens of an educator and for the purpose of compiling and advancing the understanding the research community has regarding children's spirituality in the field of education.

The search for pertinent empirical research studies, the review of relevant articles, and the analysis and compilation of all information in order to organise its presentation in this paper, was conducted over the course of several months. This search focused on expanding the work completed by Ratcliff (2010), presenting a review of scholarly studies of children's spirituality and religious development, identifying four salient phases: (1) an early holistic period (1892–1930), followed by (2) an era of decreased emphasis upon experience (1930–1960), continued by (3) three decades of emphasis upon cognitive stages (1960–1990), culminating in (4) a shift of interest towards children's spirituality (1990–2010). In Ratcliff's (2008) review of research on children's spirituality, the work completed by Robinson (1977), who examined adult retrospective accounts of their religious experiences as children; Coles (1990) findings after interviewing 500 children between 8 and 12 years old, using largely a narrative approach to compare accounts of children from different religious backgrounds; and lastly Hay and Nye's (2006) grounded theory work, looking into defining children's spirituality, arriving at the construct of relational consciousness, are highlighted as seminal works, representing the thinking in each of the decades in which they were published. The main goal of this paper is to expand on existing, yet dated, reviews of the empirical research studies on children's spirituality, looking into what has been more recently studied and published in the field, in order to better identify existing gaps and suggest avenues for future research.

In reviewing the empirical research studies published in the last 10 years, three main categories of studies arose. These categories consist of studies looking into (1) spiritual meaning-making and the relationship to/with God, (2) studies pertaining children's spirituality in education and (3) studies looking into identity formation and sense of self. The findings from this comprehensive review of the research pertaining to children's spirituality are presented below, using these three categories as the organisational framework.

Spiritual meaning-making and relations to/with god

Considered a seminal study in the field of children's spirituality, the work of Hay and Nye, conducted originally in 1998 and then revised and republished in 2006, offered a different understanding of how children make meaning of their spirituality. Using grounded theory methodology, Hay and Nye (2006) focused on 38 children between the ages of 6 and 11. These children were from different religious backgrounds and all attended a government funded, secular school in Great Britain. The researchers carried out up to three meetings with each of these children individually, tape recording their conversations and using photographs to induce spiritual talk.

They found that there are three major categories of spiritual sensitivity. These three different types of spiritual sensing refer to different realms in which children can have spiritual interactions. The first category, awareness-sensing, consists of paying attention and being alert to spiritual matters, as well as having an awareness of one's own awareness of these matters, a type of metacognitive awareness. The second category, mystery-sensing, offers children a way into the difficult area of the unknown and consists of an 'awareness of aspects of our life experience that are in principle incomprehensible' (Hay and Nye 2006, 71). By using their imagination and being in wonder and awe, children are able to tune into the mysteries of life and begin to make meaning of it. The third and last category, value-sensing, comes from a term coined by Margaret Donaldson. Donaldson criticised modern psychology for emphasising cognitive skills, while ignoring feelings and affects. In this regard, value-sensing refers to experiencing emotions and recognising feelings as a measure of what is of value (Mata 2015).

Also looking into making meaning of spirituality, Moore et al. (2011) interviewed 32 participants, ages 7–11, from various religious and cultural backgrounds, on their conceptualisation of spirituality. The parents of the participating children were asked to answer a brief demographic questionnaire, in order to provide background information on the children's religious practices and affiliated religion. Findings showed that there were common threads regarding the role of spirituality in children's lives regardless of religious background, and prayer was the most commonly discussed theme across all children's narratives, collected through semi-structured, open-ended interviews. Another prevalent theme was God's ability to help both directly and indirectly as a result of prayer.

> Gleaned from the children's voices, the present study's key themes suggest that children's thoughts and feelings about the nature of the divine, the concept of spirituality, and the purpose of prayer may help shape their perceptions of the meaning of life and aspired goals. (109)

The main contribution these two studies offer towards our understanding of how children make meaning of their spirituality lies in their ability to offer a platform to children's voices. Both of these studies allow us to 'hear' children's thoughts regarding what spirituality means to them, and how they pay attention to spiritual aspects they deem of value, as well as how they make sense of the lived experiences and practices that allow them to come to a conceptualisation of the inexplicable and of God. In this sense, these studies are groundbreaking.

Regarding the relationship to God, in 2012, Mitchell, Silver and Ross, conducted an hermeneutic phenomenological research study with 23 female Honduran youths living in residential care (foster care), between the ages of 11 and 19. Using the Lived Experience of the God–Individual Relationship Questionnaire, these young females shared their understandings and experiences of the God–individual relationship. The findings of this study showed that relationship between the individual and God, are complex and evolving. Particularly, the God–individual relationship was found to become more personal and intimate with age. The participants reported both negative and positive affective relationships. Interestingly, only participants who were 14 years-old and older indicated negative affects, signifying that younger participants only conveyed positive affects when relating their relationship with God.

In the same year, this time focusing specifically on children ages 6–11, Moore, Talwar, and Bosacki (2012), asked open-ended questions to 64 Canadian children concerning their spiritual thoughts, beliefs and experiences. The children's parents were asked to complete a demographic information questionnaire, and to report the children's religious affiliation. Regardless of children's religious background, six prominent themes emerged: (1) Positive feelings when praying or thinking about God, (2) God's location, (3) God helps, (4) God as a listener, (5) Soul and spirit and (6) God is a comforter. Their findings showed that despite diverse faith orientations, children's responses reflected similar conceptualisations of God as a listener and helper, and conversations with God served as a source of comfort and elicited feelings of happiness. Also interesting was the finding that regardless of parents describing their children as not religious at all, very few children explicitly mentioned a disbelief or skepticism about the existence of the divine. 'Moreover, all children spoke about spirituality and its role in their lives or the lives of others; even children who did not believe in a higher power' (228).

These findings parallel those of Fisher (2013) conducted with 460 Australian secondary students with diverse cultural and religious backgrounds, in which he found that relating with God provided the greatest explanation for youth's spiritual well-being (SWB). Similar findings are also noted in Fisher (2015), now looking at primary school-aged children in three different schools in Australia. Setting out to prove that using Fisher's (2004) instrument Feeling Good, Living Life (FGLL) and putting it through rigorous statistical analysis, he concludes that the FGLL is indeed a suitable instrument for investigating SWB among young children. Also, the regression analysis conducted 'showed that relating with God explains the great variance in SWB overall' (Fisher 2015, 201), emphasising the importance of the relationship with God, for children's SWB.

From these studies, it seems that regardless of the faith belief or non-belief of children, God and the child's relationship to God, tends to have a strong presence in early childhood. Spirituality, and particularly the notion of God, consistently was found to comfort and even improve children's well-being. It is also interesting to note how the studies that look into children vs. older children and adolescents, tend to convey that the younger the child the more positive their understanding of the relation they seem to have to/with God.

Children's spirituality in education

Alongside research studies looking into the relationship to/with God and how children make meaning of this relationship, there seems to be a group of studies looking into how spirituality is found and understood in the field of education. The studies composing this group focus primarily on the teachers, their views of how spirituality could be incorporated into the curriculum and how it could potentially be facilitated in classrooms (Fisher 2007; Fraser 2007; Helm, Berg, and Scranton 2008; Jacobs 2012; Hyde, 2008c; Kennedy and Duncan 2006; Mata 2012, 2013, 2014; Tan and Wong 2012). Stemming from these findings, some researchers suggest changes be made to educational policy, as well as teacher education programmes, in order to both better prepare teachers and regulate spiritual nourishment in education (Mata 2015).

In this line, Jacobs (2012) looked into teachers' views of incorporating the constructs spirituality and religion within the context of a compulsory subject in South African schools, known as Life Orientation (LO). LO attempts to teach children skills, attitudes and values from a holistic approach to human existence, and although spiritual education could be easily incorporated into this content, there are no clearly articulated policy guidelines as to how to implement it. Teachers' opinions around spirituality and LO varied, especially surrounding issues of different religious positions and questions of truth. Nevertheless, most teachers favoured the inclusion of spirituality and religion in the subject of LO, supporting the need to provide clear policy guidelines informing curriculum and providing a platform for South African teachers.

A very small, yet still available group of empirical studies look into children specifically, which is the target of this paper; trying to explain children's spirituality in relation to education. I conducted a phenomenological qualitative study with four kindergarten children, looking into describing how they experienced and expressed spirituality in the context of school (Mata 2015). In the findings of this study, I described a child's spiritual experience as

> any experience through which the child can express their joy, their compassion and kindness, their sense of relating to others and/or their creative and imaginative self. These experiences can be outwardly or inwardly triggered, and sometimes can provoke pondering and searching through inner thought and conversations; although mainly, they manifest themselves ordinarily in everyday activity. (Mata 2015, 117)

An interesting observation I came across in my study of kindergarteners' spirituality was that spirituality was expressed freely and not secretively as some scholars had suggested in the past (Hart 2003). I noted,

> the children I observed did not need permission from teachers to ponder, to ask questions, to be kind, to care for others, to connect to their surroundings, to enjoy favorite activities, to be helpful, and to be concerned. The just were. They expressed these spiritual aspects freely and without a carefully designed spiritual curriculum behind every activity and action they engaged in. (Mata 2015, 118)

Bone (2005) also explored three different early childhood settings, within a case study methodology involving the voices of children, teachers and parents, using the metaphor of 'breaking bread' to look into how spiritual experiences are nurtured around activities related to food and eating. Bone (2005) found that

> at the Steiner kindergarten children were involved in a whole cycle of food preparation from crop to compost and families were very supportive of this. In the Montessori school parents and teachers were appreciative of the attention children paid to preparing and eating food. [And] At the preschool parents realised that food was a means of connecting with children during their day and teachers saw food management as a way that children can assert their independence. (315)

From a spiritual perspective, Bone (2005) found, 'breaking bread'

> implies feeding the body and soul, having space to share and time for appreciation and social interaction, and opportunity for spiritual renewal. In the early childhood context 'breaking bread', in its symbolic and literal sense, is a way of encouraging harmony, affirming life, celebrating change, connecting with a variety of philosophical beliefs and a means of honouring the spirit of the child. (316)

Focusing on the study of slightly older children, Mountain (2007), conducted a case study methodology project in her classroom, looking into the religious education curriculum of two groups of children (25 students aged 12 years old, and 21 students aged 11 years old). Using the system of inquiry of the Melbourne Institute of Experiential and Creative Arts Therapy (MIECAT) as both a therapeutic method (based on the companioning process focused on creative arts in order to bring to better understanding unexplored areas of experience) and a research tool (using grounded theory, expanding the experience of teaching to then condensate it in keywords, clusters and themes), Mountain (2007) found that through the active engagement of imagination in the child, teachers can lead students to deeper aspects of personal understanding and knowing about themselves, their environment and the transcendent' (204). She noted, that creative arts activities engage children in learning that is intimately related to spiritual development, 'involving self-understanding, understanding relationships, wider environmental connectedness and connection with the divine (191).

Also, interviewing elementary school children, Wills (2011) set out to find proof that the magic of music indeed promotes children's well-being through singing. In open-ended interviews she conducted with six of her students (ages 9–11), she found the children reported that signing in the chorus provided a dimension that transcends the immediate, helping them forget about everything else happening at school or at home, and allowing them to express themselves and concentrate in connecting and collaborating with others to make something 'better' than can be accomplished alone. Wills proposes music facilitates spiritual experiences for children, regarding transcendence, connectedness and being in the 'flow'. The children Wills interviewed, all reported music helping them feel a sense of accomplishment and feeling happy.

Furthermore, Hyde (2008b) following an hermeneutic phenomenological approach to qualitative research, studied 12 primary aged children in 3 Australian Catholic schools. From his observations, conversations and video recording of the life expressions of these two groups of children (8–10 year-olds) (Hyde 2008c), he found four distinctive characteristics of children's spirituality: the felt sense, integrating awareness, weaving the threads of meaning and spiritual questing. He termed this last characteristic spiritual questing (Hyde 2008a) since he saw the children as 'spiritual seekers, finding authentic ways of connecting with self, other, the world, and with God' (32). In order to nurture all of these four characteristics of children's spirituality, Hyde proposes three pedagogical changes to be addressed by Australian Catholic schools: (1) the use of tactile activities in religious education, (2) the need to begin religious education with the students' personally created frameworks of meaning and (3) the need to create space to nurture spirituality, 'enabling students to weave together the threads of meaning, and to quest for authentic ways of being in the world' (Hyde 2008b, 126).

The strength and contribution of these studies to field of early childhood education, lies within the call they all make to revise the experiences children are having in schools, in order to allow for the children to be happier (Wills 2011), by taking into account children's spiritual characteristic (Hyde 2008b), honouring the spirit of the child (Bone 2005), engaging children in creative arts within religious education curricula (Jacobs 2012; Mountain 2007), while allowing children to freely experience and express their spirituality in the classrooms in which they find themselves (Mata 2015).

Identity formation and sense of self

Identity formation and sense of self is another theme also prevalent in the research found on children's spirituality. Regarding identity formation specifically, Moriarty (2011) conducted an hermeneutic phenomenological analysis of material gained from semi-structured interviews with 24 state primary school children, ages 8–10. Using a model of children's spirituality composed of four dimensions of spirituality derived from the literature: consciousness, relationality, roadmap and identity, with a central integrating concept of worldview, and Champagne's (2003) spiritual modes of being (i.e., sensitive, relational and existential). Her findings showed that these four dimensions are closely interlinked, and provided some evidence that children's spirituality progresses towards a meaningful, integrated sense of Identity. Yet, since for these children, worldview seemed to be a work in progress, and part of the Identity dimension rather than a separate construct, this led Moriarty to the production of 'a modified form of this model which provided a progressing, multidimensional conceptual framework which complements the conceptualizations of other researchers in the field of children's spirituality' (271).

Regarding gender and personal well-being, Eaude (2004) conducted in-depth observations of, and discussions with, 14 teachers of four and five-year-olds in 10 different early childhood classrooms, in mainstream schools in Oxfordshire. Within the three semi-structured discussions he had with each teacher, he began to wonder whether gender was a factor in children's spiritual development. In the meta-reflection of his findings, Eaude (2004) presents empirical evidence on aspects associated with personal well-being indicating outcomes strongly differentiated by children's gender, which he proposes need to be further looked into by researchers.

Moreover, taking two sets of data sources and collection, Gunnestad and Thwala (2011) analysed: (1) the written retrospective stories of preschool teacher students from Zambia and Swaziland, regarding a difficult time in their childhood and reflecting on what helped them cope, and (2) the answers from interviews of orphan children regarding their situation and needs. Within the analysis, the researchers set out to identify how religion affected the participants' coping skills in a crisis. They found that the opportunity to work on a crisis in cooperation with God and friends through *prayer and intercession* was a common strategy used by the participants, and it seemed 'to have created strength in the child to fight on' (Gunnestad and Thwala 2011, 183). They also found that *prayer* often operated in combination with *fellowship*, meaning that the traumatised children received moral, spiritual and practical support from Christian friends and church members. *Faith and hope* also emerged as important resources in resilience. *Prayer, fellowship* and *Word of God* had provided faith and hope to the participants in the past. *Values and good models* offered help in facing difficulties and making good choices in difficult situations. And finally, religious '*counselling* seemed to be a resource in resilience by helping the child to understand the situation, re-establish meaning and redefine the crises in a more positive way; and in that way also open up for new opportunities' (183). Gunnestad and Thwala's (2011), findings demonstrated that when religion is a central part of children and youth's worldview, as reported by the participants, it can contribute much to resilience when going through and stepping out of a crisis.

In a similar vein, when searching for correlations between happiness and spirituality, Holder, Coleman, and Wallace (2008) used the Spiritual Well-Being Questionnaire (SWBQ) 'developed by Gomez and Fisher (2003)' (Boynton 2011), and 11 items selected and modified from the Brief Multidimensional Measurement of Religiousness/Spirituality, which reflected the children's practices and beliefs, to assess 320 children 8–12 years of age, from public and private (i.e., faith-based) schools. In order to gauge children's happiness self-reports were used 'based on the Oxford Happiness Scale short form, the Subjective Happiness Scale, and a single-item measure' (131). Parents were also asked to rate their children's happiness; and temperament was similarly rated using the emotionality, activity and sociability temperament survey. From their data analysis, the researchers found that 'children's spirituality, but not their religious practices (e.g., attending church, praying, and meditating), was strongly linked to their happiness' (131). Children who were more spiritual were happier than those who were not as spiritual. Findings additionally showed that temperament was also a predictor of happiness, yet spirituality remained the significant predictor of happiness, mainly the 'personal (i.e., meaning and value in one's own life) and communal (quality and depth of inter-personal relationships) domains of spirituality were particular good predictors of children's happiness' (131).

Looking at older children and adolescents (ages 13–17), studying in Buddhist secondary schools, Yeung and Chow (2010) used semi-structured interviews to delineate the participants' religiosity regarding: '(1) the sources and resources of religiosity, (2) religious beliefs, (3) religious practices, (4) positive consequences of religiosity, and (5) predictions on the future development of religiosity' (5). The results showed that the religiosity of Buddhist adolescents in Hong Kong exhibits some special features that distinguish it from the more common understanding of religiosity in the West. The most prominent feature is the apparent absence of reference to the relationship with the transcendent or the divine. 'The adolescents repeatedly referred to the law-like objectivity of Buddhist teachings and saw the superiority of their religion in not promoting the dependence on divine help. Buddhism taught them to take up their own responsibility of life' (20); making their religious sense of self a quite independent one.

Also interesting was the finding that the commitment or connection to a particular religious community was not crucial. Thus, issues like membership or regular attendance to religious rites had no place in the religiosity of the Buddhist adolescents or did these practices influence how they understood their sense of self from a religious perspective. 'They understood their religious beliefs and practices mainly in terms of doing better in tasks like academic study, taking responsibility, controlling emotions, and building better human relationships' (21).

This group of studies emphasises the importance of spirituality in children's worldview and identity formation (Moriarty 2011), as well as presents it as a sounding mechanism for increasing happiness (Holder, Coleman, and Wallace 2008). Nevertheless, also interesting is the juxtaposition of faith and prayer as pillars for resilience during crisis (Gunnestad and Thwala 2011), vs. Buddhist youth not seeing divine properties of religion as determining, but more so giving importance to the law-like effects religion has for them in taking ownership and responsibility for their lives (Yeung and Chow 2010). These contrasting results give us pause, and forge roads towards thinking about differences within religious views and spirituality, and the impact they have on children and their understanding of how they live their spiritual selves.

Implications of findings and recommendations for future research

In reviewing the research conducted thus far in the field of children's spirituality, I agree with Ratcliff (2008), when impressed with the similarities between the first period of research and recent developments in the field, states, 'it must be admitted that the current approach to human development is far from the holism of a 100 years ago' (36). I concur that the research on children's spirituality will continue to benefit from distancing itself from developmentalist and exclusively cognitive focused views, and from approaching the study of this topic with a broader, more holistic awareness.

Aside from broadening our perspective of spirituality to a more holistic approach of researching and trying to understand these experiences, future studies need to continue to focus on children as their main participants. Retrospective studies have their value and help provide an adult understanding of experiences occurred in childhood. Yet, they are not enough. More empirical studies with the age range of the studies presented here, need to be conducted in order to truly grasp and be able to further along our understanding of what experiencing and expressing spirituality really looks like for our young children. The more we know about children's spirituality, directly from children, the better our chances to near the core of the issue, being able to better describe it, better define and better understand it. And thus, following, be better prepared to recognise, nurture and promote children's spirituality for future generations of young children.

Regarding our multicultural and diverse characteristics as a global population, I concur with Moore, Talwar, and Bosacki (2012) when they state, 'future research is needed to develop measures of spirituality that capture the diversity and breadth of children's spiritual beliefs within a multicultural context as well as measure the impact of children's spirituality on their social adjustment and coping' (232). Along these same lines, Boyatzis (2008) also calls for research that studies children's spirituality in diverse cultures and religions around the globe. He proposes the use of Bronfenbrenner (1997) social-ecological model to illuminate the many influences on children's spiritual development, by analysing diverse social contexts of growth. I agree wholeheartedly with the use of the social-ecological model. I think it will provide an appropriate and useful lens through which we can better understand children's spirituality as a complex phenomenon.

Multicultural approaches to researching children's spirituality are indeed needed, in order to better understand the complexities of this phenomenon. Yet, the term multicultural has been used in the field of education to refer to a compilation of cultures and cultural related characteristics (e.g., language, ethnicity, race, etc.) that need to be addressed in order to provide all children 'equal chance to achieve academically' (Banks and McGee Banks 2012, 1). These cultural characteristics are seen as plentiful and varied in classrooms, therefore, the use of the prefix multi in the term multicultural. Yet, do these multi-cultures interact with each other in a way that produces as an outcome a new different type of classroom culture, a product of the presence of these various characteristics? I believe it does. Thus, borrowing from Spanish, I propose introducing the term *pluricultural* view, instead of multicultural, as a focus and guiding light for the future study of children's spirituality.

A pluricultural perspective to children's spirituality will allow scholars and researchers to approach spirituality, not from the typical understanding of multiculturalism, yet from a position of endless possibilities once different cultures are present within a group of children, or within the environment surrounding a particular child. The influences of diversity and multiple cultures then do not limit themselves to just being present and acknowledged, now the researcher would need to take his or her observations to a higher level of understanding, and invent new lingo in order to describe children's pluricultural experiences and expressions of their spirituality.

Under a pluricultural lens of study, children's spirituality could be recognised across regions, and ways in which spirituality is understood and lived in both Western and Eastern societies, could be explored. Identifying tensions between individual vs. community focused views and expressions of spirituality, would allow for not only the spiritual characteristic of different regions to surface, but also to explore the inter and intra spiritual connections found in pluricultural environments. New notions of how spirituality is experienced, expressed and overall lived could be recognised and described, to help better understand the globally connected and forever changing world in which our children live.

Along with the pluricultural aspects that need to be highlighted in studies on children's spirituality, a call for more pluralistic religious view is also pertinent. Not all, yet the majority of the studies found during this review approach the research of children's spirituality from a Judeo/Christian perspective. It is important to note that various religious practices, as well as the cultural and environmental influences on these practices, need to be considered when looking at children's spirituality, especially when trying to address contemporary cultural and religious diversity, and offer global perspective to understanding how spirituality may impact meaning-making, identity, and relating to self, other and the transcendent.

In this regard, Boyatzis (2008) also calls scholars to 'move beyond a "main effects" emphasis that focuses on between group differences … and examine the *interactions* between multiple variables' (52). Stating that,

> large-scale survey studies are invaluable for charting out the basic relationships between constructs, but deeper work – ideally, in-depth qualitative work with multiple informants within these multiple social contexts – will be needed to more clearly understand the dynamics between the constructs and contexts (51). Roehlkepartain and Patel (2006) concur when stating there is a 'need for qualitative and quantitative studies that go both deep and wide' (333).

Nevertheless, when speaking of research Ratcliff (2008) reminds us, 'research is invaluable in the quest to understand children's spirituality, but even the most sophisticated investigation will produce only a partial reflection of reality (1 Cor 13:12)' (38). Thus, it is imperative that we produce an abundance of different types of research, contemplating various perspectives and many variables, in order to have access to the full picture of children's spirituality. I propose we embark in this pluricultural task, for the spiritual benefit of our young children.

Disclosure statement

No potential conflict of interest was reported by the author.

References

Allen, H. C. 2008. "Exploring Children's Spirituality from a Christian Perpective." In *Nurturing Children's Spirituality: Christian Perspectives and Best Practices*, edited by H. C. Allen, 5–20. Eugene, OR: Cascade Books.
Andrews, C. R., and S. A. Marotta. 2005. "Spirituality and Coping among Grieving Children: A Preliminary Study." *Counseling and Values* 50: 38–50.

Austin, J. 2000. "Consciousness Evolves When Self Dissolves." In *Cognitive Models and Spiritual Maps: Interdisciplinary Explorations of Religious Experience*, edited by J. Andresen and R. Forman, 209–30. Thorverton, UK: Imprint Academic.

Banks, J. A., and C. A. McGee Banks, eds. 2012. *Multicultural Education: Issues and Perspectives*. 8th ed. Hoboken, NJ: Wiley.

Bone, J. 2005. "Breaking Bread: Spirituality, Food and Early Childhood Education." *International Journal of Children's Spirituality* 10 (3): 307–317.

Boyatzis, C. J. 2008. "Children's Spiritual Development: Advancing the Field in Definition, Measurement, and Theory." In *Nurturing Children's Spirituality: Christian Perspectives and Best Practices*, edited by H. C. Allen, 43–57. Eugene, OR: Cascade Books.

Boynton, H. M. 2011. "Children's Spirituality: Epistemology and Theory from Various Helping Professions." *International Journal of Children's Spirituality* 16 (2): 109–127.

Bronfenbrenner, U. 1997. *The Ecology of Human Development*. Cambridge, MA: Harvard University Press.

Champagne, E. 2003. "Being a Child, a Spiritual Child." *International Journal of Children's Spirituality* 8 (1): 43–53.

Coles, R. 1990. *The Spiritual Life of Children*. Boston, MA: Houghton Mifflin Company.

Dewey, J. 1938. *Experience & Education*. New York: Touchstone.

Eaude, T. 2004. "Do Young Boys and Girls Have Distinct and Different Approaches and Needs in Relation to Spiritual Development?" *International Journal of Children's Spirituality* 9 (1): 53–66.

Fisher, J. 2004. "Feeling Good, Living Life: A Spiritual Health Measure for Young Children." *Journal of Beliefs and Values* 25 (3): 307–315.

Fisher, J. W. 2007. "It's Time to Wake up and Stem the Decline in Spiritual Well-being in Victorian Schools." *International Journal of Children's Spirituality* 12 (2): 165–177.

Fisher, J. 2013. "Assessing Spiritual Well-Being: Relating with God Explains Greatest Variance in Spiritual Well-being among Australian Youth." *International Journal of Children's Spirituality* 18 (4): 306–317.

Fisher, J. W. 2015. "God Counts for Children's Spiritual Well-being." *International Journal of Children's Spirituality* 20 (3–4): 191–203.

Fraser, D. 2007. "State Education, Spirituality, and Culture: Teachers' Personal and Professional Stories of Negotiating the Nexus." *International Journal of Children's Spirituality* 12 (3): 289–305.

Gomez, R., and J. W. Fisher. 2003. "Domains of Spiritual Well-Being and Development of Validation of the Spiritual Well-Being Questionnaire." *Personality and Individual Differences* 35 (8): 1975–1991.

Gunnestad, A., and S'I. Thwala. 2011. "Resilience and Religion in Children and Youth in Southern Africa." *International Journal of Children's Spirituality* 16 (2): 169–185.

Hart, T. 2003. *The Secret Spiritual World of Children*. Makawao, HI: Inner Ocean Publishing.

Hay, D., and R. Nye. 2006. *The Spirit of the Child*. Revised ed. London: Jessica Kingsley.

Helm, J. H., S. Berg, and P. Scranton. 2008. "Documenting Children's Spiritual Development in a Preschool Program." In *Nurturing Children's Spirituality: Christian Perspectives and Best Practices*, edited by H. C. Allen, 214–229. Eugene, OR: Cascade Books.

Holder, M. D., B. Coleman, and J. Wallace. 2008. "Spirituality, Religiousness, and Happiness in Children Aged 8–12 Years." *Journal of Happiness Studies* 11: 131–150.

Hyde, B. 2008a. "I Wonder What You Think Really, Really Matters? Spiritual Questing and Religious Education." *Religious Education* 103 (1): 32–47.

Hyde, B. 2008b. "The Identification of Four Characteristics of Children's Spirituality in Australian Catholic Primary Schools." *International Journal of Children's Spirituality* 13 (2): 117–127.

Hyde, B. 2008c. "Weaving the Threads of Meaning: A Characteristic of Children's Spirituality and Its Implications for Religious Education." *British Journal of Religious Education* 30 (3): 235–245.

Jacobs, A. C. 2012. "South African Teachers' Views on the Inclusion of Spirituality Education in the Subject Life Orientation." *International Journal of Children's Spirituality* 17 (3): 235–253.

Kennedy, A., and J. Duncan. 2006. "New Zealand Children's Spirituality in Catholic Schools: Teachers' Perspectives." *International Journal of Children's Spirituality* 11 (2): 281–292.

Lewis, J. 2000. "Spiritual Education as the Cultivation of Qualities of the Heart and Mind. A Reply to Blake and Carr." *Oxford Review of Education* 26: 263–283.

Mata, J. 2012. "Nurturing Spirituality in Early Childhood Classrooms: The Teacher's View." In *Spirituality: Theory, Praxis and Pedagogy*, edited by M. Fowler, J. D. Martin, and J. L. Hochheimer, 239–248. Oxford: Inter-Disciplinary Press.

Mata, J. 2013. "Meditation: Using It in the Classroom." In *Spirituality in the 21st Century: Journeys beyond Entrenched Boundaries*, edited by W. V. Moer, D. A. Celik, and J. L. Hochheimer, 109–119. Oxford: Inter-Disciplinary Press.

Mata, J. 2014. "Sharing My Journey and Opening Spaces: Spirituality in the Classroom." *International Journal of Children's Spirituality* 19 (2): 112–122.

Mata, J. 2015. *Spiritual Experiences in Early Childhood Education: Four Kindergarteners, One Classroom*. New York: Routledge.

Mitchell, M. B., C. F. Silver, and C. J. Ross. 2012. "My Hero, My Friend: Exploring Honduran Youths' Lived Experience of the God-individual Relationship." *International Journal of Children's Spirituality* 17 (2): 137–151.

Moore, K., V. Talwar, and S. Bosacki. 2012. "Canadian Children's Perceptions of Spirituality: Diverse Voices." *International Journal of Children's Spirituality* 17 (3): 217–234.

Moore, K., V. Talwar, S. Bosacki, and J. Park-Saltzman. 2011. "Diverse Voices: Children's Perceptions of Spirituality." *Alberta Journal of Educational Research* 57 (1): 107–110.

Moriarty, M. W. 2011. "A Conceptualization of Children's Spirituality Arising out of Recent Research." *International Journal of Children's Spirituality* 16 (3): 271–285. doi:http://dx.doi.org/10.1080/1364436X.2011.617730.

Mountain, V. 2007. "Educational Contexts for the Development of Children's Spirituality: Exploring the Use of Imagination." *International Journal of Children's Spirituality* 12 (2): 191–205.

Newberg, A., E. d'Aquili, and V. Rause. 2001. *Why God Won't go Away: Brain Science and the Biology of Belief*. New York: Ballantine.

Ratcliff, D. 2008. "'The Spirit of Children's past': A Century of Children's Spirituality Research." In *Nurturing Children's Spirituality: Christian Perspectives and Best Practices*, edited by H. C. Allen, 21–42. Eugene, OR: Cascade Books.

Ratcliff, D. 2010. "Children's Spirituality: Past and Future." *Journal of Spiritual Formation & Soul Care* 3 (1): 6–20.

Robinson, E. 1977. *The Original Vision: A Study of the Religious Experience of Childhood*. Oxford: The Religious Experience Research Center.

Roehlkepartain, E. C., and E. Patel. 2006. "Congregations: Unexamined Crucibles for Spiritual Development." In *The Handbook of Spiritual Development in Childhood and Adolescence*, edited by E. C. Roehlkepartain, P. E. King, L. Wagener, and P. L. Benson, 324–336. Thousand Oaks, CA: Sage.

de Souza, M. 2004. "Teaching for Effective Learning in Religious Education: A Discussion of the Perceiving, Thinkoing, Feeling and Intuitive Elements in the Learning Process." *Journal of Religious Education* 52 (3): 22–30.

Taggart, G. 2001. "Nurturing Spirituality: A Rationale for Holistic Education." *International Journal of Children's Spirituality* 6 (3): 325–339.

Tan, C., and Y. Wong. 2012. "Promoting Spiritual Ideals through Design Thinking in Public Schools." *International Journal of Children's Spirituality* 17 (1): 25–37.

Wills, R. 2011. "The Magic of Music: A Study into the Promotion of Children's Well-being through Singing." *International Journal of Children's Spirituality* 16 (1): 37–46.

Yeung, G. K. K., and W. Chow. 2010. "'To Take up Your Own Responsibility': The Religiosity of Buddhist Adolescents in Hong Kong." *International Journal of Children's Spirituality* 15 (1): 5–23.

Yust, K., A. N. Johnson, S. E. Sasso, and E. C. Roehlkepartian, eds. 2006. *Nurturing Child and Adolescent Spirituality: Perspectives from the World's Religious Traditions*. Lahan, MD: Rowman and Littlefield.

ə OPEN ACCESS

Navigating the spaces of children's spiritual experiences: influences of tradition(s), multidisciplinarity and perceptions

Kate Adams

ABSTRACT
Children across the world report similar spiritual experiences. Empirical studies suggest that most resonate with the children's traditions; a finding which should, in theory, afford them a safe spiritual space. However, a number of factors can situate them in a less certain place. The paper uses the metaphors of trees imbued with different shades of light, from the vivid, shimmering and opaque to the invisible, to illustrate the types of spiritual spaces in which children find themselves. Their location is shaped in part by connection or disconnection with traditions, alongside wider cultural forces. Three navigation tools are used to show how children may move between these spaces: the spiritual experience and its relationship with traditions; the influences of multidisciplinary approaches; and children's perceptions of their experiences. The paper concludes that these metaphors and tools may be a useful way to understand the spiritual spaces in which children find themselves.

Introduction

A spiritual experience or encounter can be an intense and impactful moment in a child's life, often shaping their beliefs long into adulthood. They may manifest as an occasional yet pivotal event or as a more regular occurrence embedded in the routine of daily life. Examples include an intense dream believed to bring a divine communication; a sighting of a deceased loved one; a meeting with a divine being; a constant companion unseen by others usually known as an 'imaginary friend'; a guardian angel who sits beside a child's bed each night to protect them whilst they sleep; or, for a small minority, a near-death experience (Adams 2010; see also Rankin 2008 for a more extensive list oriented towards adults' experiences).

All of the aforementioned children's experiences are represented in various, sometimes disparate, literatures including the academic (e.g. Coles 1990; Robinson 1996; Hoffman 1992; Hart 2003; Scott 2004; Hay and Nye 2006; Adams, Hyde, and Woolley 2008; Potgieter, van der Walt, and Wolhuter 2009; Pettersen

2015; Lovelock and Adams 2017) and the commercial/Mind Body Spirit genres (e.g. Newcomb 2008). Some experiences take the form of systematic studies whilst others appear as illustrative narratives in wider discourses on children's spirituality; some are focussed on one type of experience such as dreams (e.g. Potgieter, van der Walt, and Wolhuter 2009); others are adult recollections (e.g. Hoffman 1992; Scott 2004); whilst some studies engage directly with children about a range of experiences (e.g. Coles 1990). However, despite their different approaches, collectively they offer significant insights into children's experiences and in so doing, provide a doorway into exploring how tradition(s) and culture(s) shape and influence both the encounter itself and adults and children's interpretation of it.

This paper presents an original contribution to the field by exploring the relationship between children's spiritual experiences and traditions through the lens of space – the spiritual spaces which the children and traditions occupy and the fluidity of those spaces. Using the metaphors of trees enveloped in different shades of light, the paper argues that a child can inhabit various spaces along a continuum, from vivid spaces which afford certainty and confidence through to an invisible space, undetectable to others, which may effectively erase the experience from existence.

The children's journeys through these spaces are explored through the influences of three key elements which can serve as navigation tools to understand their positioning within a space:

- The nature of the children's spiritual experience and the relationship with traditions;
- The influence of multidisciplinary approaches on understanding experiences and shaping spaces;
- The children's perceptions of their experiences.

As the paper works through these elements to illustrate the nature of the different spaces and their complexities, conflicts and tensions, each is exemplified by empirical evidence from various studies. This process of exemplification affords children their spiritual voice(s) – voices which often go unheard. The metaphors for these spaces are interwoven throughout these sections to illustrate how children may move in-between them. This is undertaken with the overarching aim of offering an original and accessible framework within which to better understand how children might find themselves positioned in the world of spiritual experiences. This framework may be useful for a range of academics and practitioners in the field, including those in education, social work, chaplaincy, arts and psychology.

Metaphors: trees and light

The central metaphors for these spaces are trees – and children – imbued with different shades of light and darkness. Trees are chosen for their integral connection with the earth, as life-giving and symbolic of both growth and death. A feature of many myths and religious scriptures the world over, the tree has long represented a myriad of spiritual ideas. These include the Tree of Wisdom under which Buddha achieved enlightenment, the Tree of Knowledge in the Biblical creation narrative, and Yyggdrasill, the World Tree, which links earth and heaven and all life according to Norse mythology (Greene and Sharman-Burke 1999). The connection between trees and the spiritual world is also found in Celtic, Swedish and Japanese mythologies as well as those of Ancient Greece and Rome where they were believed to be the home of the Dryads (nymphs) (New World Encyclopedia 2015). Light is a symbol which is widespread through religions. Becker (Becker 2000, 177) notes that it represents God, spirit, the immaterial, life and happiness. Furthermore, it is 'frequently encountered as a border of darkness', which can indicate mystery, misfortune or 'spiritual dullness.'

In addition, these metaphors have also been chosen because of their relevance to children. Trees, forests and light and dark are all familiar symbols to children, presented to them from an early age through stories in books and other media such as film or video games. Fairy tales provide a traditional source of these symbols; Gadd (2014) notes how heroes and heroines of fairy tales are often trapped in forests in darkness, where they need to overcome evil to reach the light.

Furthermore, as will be discussed later, the notion of dark spirituality (de Souza 2012) is highly pertinent to the field and requires further exploration; darkness is thus a relevant metaphor here too. The metaphors, which are embedded in the following images (Figures 1–4), may therefore have the potential to also be used with and by children, who may be able to recognise themselves in the relevant spaces. In so doing, the paper offers an original approach, based on research, to enabling adults and children to visualise and describe their positioning in relation to a spiritual experience.

Figure 1 depict the image of a child sitting against a majestic, ancient tree, drenched in strong sunlight. The figurerepresents the most vivid of spaces in which we might expect that a tradition(s) and wider culture should, arguably, give children a solid grounding. It is symbolised by a strong, old tree whose roots dig deep and wide, affirming its lineage, anchored to the earth for sustenance, as it simultaneously reaches up towards the heavens, providing home for wildlife and offering shade and protection. Here, the child should find a secure home: a safe haven under which to sit, back rested against the bark of the trunk, supported by it and protected by the canopy of the hanging branches. The space is brightly illuminated yet leaves filter the life-giving sunlight, also giving sanctuary from the falling rain as their tradition(s) validates their experience.

PERSPECTIVES ON CHILDREN'S SPIRITUALITY IN DIVERSE AND CHANGING CONTEXTS

Figure 1. The vivid space.

Photo was taken by Soloway/123RF. Stock photo. https://www.123rf.com/photo_43192171_little-boy-reading-a-book-under-big-linden-tree.html?term=boy%2Bsitting%2Breading%2Blinden%2Btree&vti=lbbtw8uz03r8ljdmau-1-2Accessed 14 October 2018

In this vivid space, the child has confidence and clarity in their experience and understanding of it, supported by the tradition(s) and culture(s) to which they belong.

Figure 2 illustrates the second image, that of a protective canopy under which a child is further supported as they walk towards a brighter light offering increasing insight and clarity. The sunshine glimmers through the leaves, shedding light on the pathway taken by the child and their companion. The image represents the shimmering space, whose light imbues different qualities of openness, questioning and enquiry. The child is accompanied by a supportive other who, irrespective of their opinions of the veracity of the experience, is conscious of the need to respect the child's views. The traditions and wider cultural influences may or may not correlate in their entirety, but there is a sufficient underpinning for the child to feel validated and nurtured on their journey to making meaning.

Figure 2. The shimmering space.

Photo was taken by Lorraine Cormier. CC0 Creative Commons, free for commercial use. https://pixabay.com/en/father-son-walk-child-boy-family-2770301/ Accessed 1 September 2018

In this nurtured space, with the warmth of the shimmering light, the child is not alone, finding support from others and/or their traditions. Perhaps with some doubts or questions, they nevertheless feel comfortable to share them with others, enquire and express any doubts freely without fearing judgement.

Figure 3 illustrates the opaque space, seeing the darkness slowly descending, altering the visibility of the tree. The image represents the opaque space in which the tree's shape is clearly recognisable but a little less tangible to the naked eye as the light fades. The shadows cast by the ensuing dusk obscures its silhouette a little, and that of the child, in some cases indicative of apprehension, anxiety or fear.

In this opaque space, with light becoming blocked, some uncertainty may have crept in. Any underpinning tradition(s) is still present, but the dimming light casts some doubt and/or disconnect. A confusion, perhaps emanating from conflicting perspectives, gives rise to a child's introspection and a sense of liminality, with no obvious person to turn to for guidance and support.

The final image (Figure 4) sees the trees descending into the mists. The picture represents the invisible space in which the sight of the previously tangible tree, once so clear in the intense sunlight, fades rapidly into obscurity. Alongside its neighbouring trees, it still exists, but its downwards roots and upwards links to the heavens are enveloped in the swirling fog as its visibility dissipates.

The child too has dissolved into the mist, disappearing from sight; others' disinterest, doubt, cynicism or outright rejection have weighed heavily, and the tradition(s) become so far removed, that both the child and their encounter drift into invisibility, as if the experience had never taken place.

Figure 3. The opaque space.

Photo was taken by StockSnap. CC0 Creative Commons, free for commercial use. https://pixabay.com/get/eb30b60d29f4043ed1534705fb0938c9bd22ffd41cb218409cf9c879a5/people-2572105_1920.jpg?attachment Accessed 1 September 2018

Figure 4. The invisible space.
Photo was taken by Stefan Schweihofer. CCO Creative Commons, free for commercial use.https://pixabay.com/en/fog-pine-trees-mysterious-571786/ Accessed 1 September 2018

These Figures 1-4 and spaces are not intended to be exhaustive or restrictive in their categorisations, but rather symbolic of different spaces which children may commonly find themselves situated in. Throughout the subsequent interrogation of the influences of three key navigation tools on children's spiritual experiences, these figures are interwoven to illustrate how the themes can potentially impact on the spiritual space or spaces which a child may inhabit.

The nature of children's spiritual experience and the relationship with traditions

Notwithstanding the fact that the literature on children's spiritual experiences is still a developing area, as noted above, the various literatures suggest that even when children from different countries and cultures share similar experiences, there is a tendency for them to be mostly rooted in their respective traditions. This first navigation tool is intended to provide insight into the importance of this relationship, which is illustrated by two specific types: encounters with angels, and dreams with a perceived divine connection.

First, children's encounters with angels are a common reccurrence across different studies (see examples in Hoffman 1992; Hart 2003; Newcomb 2008; Adams 2010; Pettersen 2015; Lovelock and Adams 2017). Pettersen's (2015) enquiries with children aged 3–5 in Canada elicited descriptions conforming to Christian imagery of angels, with faces, bodies, wings and halos. In all but two references, children referred to them as female. Pettersen (2015) also found that most referred to angels as family members (mostly female and usually their mother), assigning them a nurturing role, consonant with the western concept of the guardian angel. The alignment with gender and family members was also present in Newcomb's (2008) work, who noted that children reported angels taking different forms according to the nature of the situation. For example, when the child needed healing, the angel was often reported as taking a female form, and when the child needed protection, the angel was said to assume the appearance of a warrior.

The concept of the guardian angel, combined with the depiction of a human form with wings, was also observed by Hart writing in the USA (2003), my work in the UK (Adams 2010) and that of Newcomb (2008), who collected narratives from around the world. For these children the alignment with the Christian tradition (even if the children were not Christian themselves) may place them initially in a vivid space: what they report is consonant with their respective country's underpinning historical traditions and contemporary cultural images. As Underhill (1995) observes, whilst Ancient Greek and Roman art depicted winged figures with human bodies, there was no separation between gods and the natural world; the gods came to earth, with no significant need for intermediary messengers. It was not until the earliest Christian art that angels were portrayed as adult males, and as time progressed, artists began to ascribe them wings and halos.

Today, such 'traditionally' Christian images of winged beings are propagated through cartoons, Christmas cards, internet, social media and adverts – embedded in both religious and secular cultures alike. Whilst children report angels taking different appearances, such as family members (see Newcomb 2008; Pettersen 2015), this image still resonates with the earlier Protestant notions and contemporary wider cultural narratives such as angels taking the form of a human being who arrives to offer help. Hence, where children's reports of angels resonate with such depictions, they potentially find themselves in a vivid space.

A second example of where experiences are similar across different groups of children, but also resonate with respective traditions, lies with children's divine dreams; these are dreams in sleep which the child believes has a divine source and/or in which the child encountered a divine being. This type of dream has a rich heritage in traditions across the world from ancient civilisations such as Egypt, Greece and China through to the Judaeo-Christian and Islamic faiths (Bulkeley 2008). Inherent in these traditions is the belief that the divine uses dreams as a vehicle for communicating with humans.

Whilst studies into the experiences of adults who report this type of dream have been ongoing for decades (e.g. Charsley 1973; Azam 1992; Curley 1992), those with children have been far fewer. This is despite the fact that these dreams have been highly significant for some children, and more often experienced than may be generally realised.

In my larger investigation, I questioned 505 children from Christian, Muslim and secular children aged 9–12 to ask if they had ever had a divine dream. Of those, 109 (22%) children reported at least one, and the dreams had many commonalities in their themes including precognition, instruction, warning and reassurance.

All conformed in some way (e.g. dream type, content, or interpretation of the dream) to findings in either psychological studies of dreams and/or to dreams recorded in the Hebrew Bible, New Testament and Quran and/or Hadith, respectively. However, it was noticeable that any specific imagery pertaining to religious beliefs conformed closely to the child's respective cultural background: mosques only appeared in Muslim children's dreams; only Christian or secular children dreamt of a church; and only Christian or secular children dreamt of God as a bearded man. For all of these children, their location may have been in a vivid space. This is not surprising, although several children from these different backgrounds shared the same classrooms, neighbourhoods and friendships, all seeing mosques and churches as they went about their daily lives. Furthermore, most learnt about major world religions in compulsory Religious Education lessons, often in the same classroom.

The alignment of imagery perhaps, therefore, represents a much deeper relationship with tradition which goes beyond the more superficial cultural environment. In a study with 260 children aged 12–13 in South Africa, Potgieter, van der Walt, and Wolhuter (2009) elicited similar findings with 19% (n = 49) reporting a divine dream. Similar themes to those in my UK study were evident, such as precognition, instruction and reassurance. However, there were some differences in their work which may represent differences between UK and South African cultures and traditions, such as fear of an eternity without God and fear of God's wrath.

In these examples of angels and dreams, there was clear alignment between the individuals' traditions and their experience. However, even when an encounter falls outside of their own tradition, the relationship to their environment is usually clear. For example, Hyde (2008) – in a wider study – explored children's spirituality in Catholic primary schools in Australia. He found that whilst children clearly drew on their Catholic heritage when discussing spiritual and religious matters, there were also examples of influences outside their faith background shaping their experience and understanding of the events, such as reincarnation and astrology. This convergence enabled children to make sense of their experiences (Hyde 2008). In this way, for some children, the experience sits in a liminal space between different, sometimes unrelated traditions, albeit that they converge only via passing references on the internet, a conversation, a mention in a book or in a Religious Education lesson in school.

Hyde's (2008) Australian study exemplifies that it is not only crossovers of different religious traditions which occur, but also combinations of the secular and 'spiritual-but-not-religious', such as 'new age' and 'mind, body, spirit' ideas which can create and influence children's spaces, perhaps moving them from a vivid space into one of the other, less clear spaces. A lack of clarity is particularly the case when mind, body, spirit notions are involved, for they are often drawn from spiritual traditions from around the world. One example is the increasing popularity in the west of eastern practices such as mindfulness. A child may not need to have a full understanding of a religious and/or spiritual concept; rather, they might only have briefly come into contact with an idea which resonates with them in order to give meaning to their experience.

The influences of multidisciplinarity on understanding encounters and shaping spaces

The field of spirituality, by its very nature, draws on work from different disciplines including religion, philosophy, theology, psychology, sociology, education, arts, social work, etc., although many authors elect to locate their work only in one discipline. In this second navigation tool, first I will use the divine dream to demonstrate how using multidisciplinary approaches to studying children's spiritual experiences provides insights into a phenomenon. At the same time, the underlying principles of working with and learning from different disciplines can also create as many certainties as uncertainties, thereby influencing the spaces in which children find themselves. Secondly, in this section, I consider multidisciplinary approaches more broadly to show how different explanations of spiritual phenomena can affect the spaces children find themselves in.

As noted earlier, divine dreams have a long history, having been recorded since ancient times (Bulkeley 2008). Their roots are therefore firmly in religion and for many believers, a divine dream needs no further explanation or validation. The respective holy text or other teaching may be entirely sufficient to anchor their experience in a vivid space.

Psychoanalysts, however, bring a different element to the conversation. For Freud (1900/1999), children's dreams were simply manifest (undisguised) wish fulfilment. Should a child dream of God, a Freudian view would thus interpret the dream as a desire to communicate with God or a father figure. Taking a Jungian (1936/1969) psychoanalytical approach would draw more deeply on the meanings of dream symbols and archetypes, and include Jung's recognition that many 'big dreams' – those which have a significant impact at the time and a lasting effect on a child (or adult) – also often have numinous qualities (Adams 2003).

In contrast, for a neuroscientist such as Hobson (1992), the content of a dream has been generated by the random firing of neurons. In his view, any patterns or meaning attributed to a dream are placed upon it afterwards by the waking brain.

Where an individual subscribes to one particular theory, tradition or discipline, they are afforded a vivid space in which to experience and reflect upon it. It provides reassurance and grounding. Yet multidisciplinarity provides different perspectives and layers for exploring spiritual experiences, some of which will be deeply contested, particularly by the person reporting the experience. Nowhere more so than in spirituality or religion is this contestation evident. For example, an adult Christian who believes that a particular dream was a communication from God, may well respect the neuroscientific or psychoanalytic explanations and even adhere to one of them to account for the majority of their dreams. However, they may reject those theories in the case of this unique dream, which they believe to be fundamentally different in essence and source to their others.

In addition to multidisciplinary approaches, one intention of interdisciplinary approaches is to explore how different stances, methodologies and evidence might converge to move thinking and outcomes forward. In the spiritual and religious arena, there are constantly evolving discussions as evidenced in the emerging field of neurotheology, which explores the relationship between the brain and religion (see Sayadmansour 2014). Furthermore, wider discussions are played out in the public arena in high profile debates on the relationship between science and religion by protagonists such as Richard Dawkins (see Dawkins 2017).

Such discourses, of course, also filter into everyday conversations and influence adults and children's thinking about spiritual experiences. A particular example comes from psychiatry which may, depending on other symptoms, associate seeing things which others can't, and hearing voices which others can't, as indicators of mental illnesses. In this medical model, having visual hallucinations may be recognised as a symptom of bipolar disorder, substance abuse or personality disorders (Mental Health Foundation 2018a) whilst auditory hallucinations may fall within a diagnosis of schizophrenia depending on other indicators (Mental Health Foundation 2018b). That said, such experiences are also recognised within psychology and psychiatry as symptoms of the grieving process when the subject of the experience relates to a deceased person (ibid). However, many health professionals agree that not all who report seeing, hearing, smelling or being touched by someone or something which no-one else is aware of are necessarily suffering from mental ill-health (Mind 2016; Rethink Mental Illness 2016). In a study of 6–18 years old (n = 95) in the Netherlands, who were attending a clinic for support with auditory visual hallucinations, researchers found that whilst all suffered from stress, only 11.6% had a psychotic disorder (Maijer, Palmen, and Sommer 2017). The complexity of this relationship between mental illness and religious and spiritual experience is beyond the scope of this paper, but is highlighted as an issue which affects adults' responses to children's reports.

For adults, these discussions about how spiritual experiences might be interpreted can be complex. Adults' views, and perhaps their own confusion emanating from such alternative explanations, are often detected by children and can lead to a move from the vivid space to one of the others. But it is not only adults' interpretations that are essential in creating the space: what of younger children who are not fully aware of these different disciplinary approaches?

The children's perceptions of their experiences

This third navigation tool firmly places the child and their spiritual voice(s) at the centre of the conversation. Children are soon alerted to the fact that many adults and peers are sceptical or dismissive of their experiences (Hart 2003;

Scott 2004; Hay and Nye 2006; Lovelock and Adams 2017). Phrases such as 'it's just your imagination', often framed innocently, can nevertheless place a fragment of doubt into a vivid space. An experience which might have been intensely profound, meaningful and 'real' to the child can be viewed differently (as within a multidisciplinary approach): they realise that it can also be interpreted as a figment of their imagination, a chemical reaction in the brain, or a trick of the mind.

Whilst not refuting the importance of critical reflection on any experience, such alternative explanations can influence the spiritual space which children occupy, potentially moving it from a vivid space through to the invisible depending on the power of the alternative explanation and potential lack of endorsement which could counter the alternatives.

How then, do children inhabit and navigate these spaces of unseen worlds, and negotiate the implications of multidisciplinarity which are presented to them in the form of different viewpoints? The immediate experiential space is usually lucid in terms of its authenticity; children's pragmatic descriptions to researchers demonstrate clarity in recall and articulate responses to questions (see accounts in Hart 2003; Pettersen 2015; Lovelock and Adams 2017).

Children are, by virtue of their cultural context, embedded in their experience in a way that is likely to resonate with other similar encounters. When a child's account is affirmed, and they remain confident in the experience, they can bask in the sunlight of the vivid space; a space underpinned by culture and tradition which can potentially support them for a lifetime. These are evident in adult recollections of childhood experiences such as Rankin's (2008) narratives drawn from the Alister Hardy archives of religious and spiritual experiences. One man told of two profound experiences from childhood which impacted on him through his life; in the first, he found himself 'surrounded, embraced by a white light, which seemed to both come from within [him] and from without... [feeling] an overwhelming sense of love, of warmth, peace and joy'. Sometime soon after, he felt compelled to take a walk, follow a specific route, and offer help to a woman who was trimming a hedge. This initiated a close and enduring friendship and he later came to call her his 'second mother'. He described the two encounters as 'really opening [him] to the significance of the spiritual dimension' and being receptive to a greater power which remained into adult life (pp. 96–98). (Also see Hoffman 1992 and Scott 2004 for further examples of adult recollections with lasting impact).

In addition, the actual fear of anticipated ridicule or dismissal is a fundamental driver in creating opaque and invisible spaces. The fear of dismissal, as well as the very act of it, can shift the child from the place of certainty about the experience to a space of doubt; doubt as to whether or not the encounter was real but also to a space in which no one appears to be validating it, where speaking about it seems to be unwelcome or unwise. Children thus find themselves in a strange hinterland, one which can move back to being vivid through the shimmering space, when an open-minded adult appears (perhaps a trusted relative, family friend, religious leader, teacher or sometimes the researcher) and the child knows that their views will be respected.

The potential darkness of a space is also important to acknowledge. Whilst the majority of children's experiences are positive, some are not and they can create and leave feelings of fear and anxiety. As de Souza (2012) and Pettersen (2015) state, and I have argued elsewhere (Adams 2010; Lovelock and Adams 2017), fears embedded in dark spirituality need to be recognised by adults and addressed. Adults sometimes tend to, with the best intentions, dismiss the experiences as imagination in order to pacify their children. However, as Pettersen (2015) states, 'Telling a child that they did not really see an angel, a ghost or deceased loved one, or even a scary monster, is making too little of their concern, and it is not for adults to decide what a child sees or how a child feels about it' (214).

When a child has been frightened by an experience, this can conversely place them in any of the spaces, even a vivid one. The vividness might not always represent positivity. It might reflect an absolute certainty about the reality of an experience, but that experience might be a frightening one. The child may have no doubts that they were, for example, visited by God in a dream and admonished for bad behaviour (see Potgieter, van der Walt, and Wolhuter 2009) – and be scared by it. An adult's response might be to reassure them that it was 'just a dream'. In such a case, this could have a positive effect, moving them to a shimmering space, which would be a much more reassuring place to be on this occasion. Yet if adults ignore the darkness, a child could remain trapped and unsupported in an invisible space.

Reflections on spiritual spaces, non-linear journeys and tradition(s)

The importance of the spiritual space(s) which a child inhabits is not to be underestimated, for it can affect their beliefs, confidence and openness for a lifetime. As noted above, whilst a child can inhabit different spiritual spaces in relation to the same spiritual experience, this movement does not necessarily have to be linear as the spaces crossed do not need to be side by side: a child who is secure in their vivid space may feel emotionally rejected by a dismissive statement from another, and find themselves withdrawing into the invisible space, no longer prepared to air it again. For example, in Scott's (2004) study of adult recollections of childhood experiences, he details the case of Rita who had experienced dreams of negative events about other people since childhood. Some of the dreams proved to be predictive and during childhood, Rita experienced 'fear or dread… of dreaming' (72). This situation would have placed her perhaps in an opaque space for she experienced confusion about them, never sure which might manifest and which might come to nothing. With a supportive adult, Rita might have been able to move into the shimmering space – with more light being shed on the phenomenon to help her understand the nature of the dreams. Instead, when she was 10 years old, her grandmother closed down all conversations about a series of nightmares and sleepwalking episodes which accurately predicted that her friend would be injured if she continued playing fairy games in a nearby forest. Into adulthood, Rita has remained in an opaque space because of this, noting that her continued dread of dreaming may 'relate to not being heard as a child' (Scott 2004, 72).

The spaces are not intended to be hierarchical. Whilst a vivid space might initially appear to be the ideal, it is not intended to be automatically afforded the highest status. Certainly, if a child is confident in the veracity of their experience and it is valued and respected by peers and traditions, this is to be welcomed. It is an illustration of respect for the child. Yet this comment comes with the recognition that certainty can also be aligned with extremist religious/ spiritual convictions which are potentially harmful. Furthermore, sometimes there is value in not being completely certain. Some doubt over an experience may be seen as a positive in that it initiates reflection and questioning of self and tradition(s). Irrespective of the outcome of such questioning, the process itself can be a valuable spiritual journey.

Conversely, the invisible space may initially appear to be the least ideal. Indeed, in most cases it is, rendering the child's experience inconsequential, airbrushing it out of any visible history even if it had conformed to religious and/or spiritual traditions. Such an impact on the child is potentially damaging, and something to be avoided at all costs; but it should be noted that some children may be content to have their experience go unnoticed. Spirituality can be intensely personal and whilst many children (and adults alike) do not express their views or experiences because they fear ridicule or dismissal, others elect not to share because they want to keep it private. A child can thus deliberately seek out invisibility for this reason, and reside happily in that space.

Finally, the influence of tradition(s) and wider cultural forces on the spaces can also be complex. On the surface, we might perceive adults' negative responses to children's experiences which are consistent with their own tradition as a personal disconnect from, or alternative interpretation to, their own tradition. Perhaps the adult considers, for example, a scriptural text on angelic experience as allegory rather than representative of lived experience; for some adults, their response may reflect a personal questioning of their tradition's validity; for others, the tradition in which they were raised may only resonate at a superficial level rather than as a deep, embedded belief.

Conclusion

A child's spiritual encounter can be a deeply meaningful experience which can confirm, challenge or further impact their beliefs and worldviews and the nature of the space which they inhabit. Any response, from an adult or peer, can further influence that positioning in a space. The three tools used here to navigate influences on the spaces – the nature of the children's spiritual experience and the relationship with tradition(s), the influences of multidisciplinarity and children's perceptions of their experiences – are not intended to be exhaustive. However, they offer an insight into how traditions and wider cultural influences can interact to shape children's spiritual spaces. With their different shades of light, from the vivid, shimmering, opaque to the invisible, these may be useful metaphors to help both adults and children understand the spaces within which children find themselves.

Disclosure statement

No potential conflict of interest was reported by the author.

References

Adams, K. 2003. "Children's Dreams: An Exploration of Jung's Concept of Big Dreams." *International Journal of Children's Spirituality* 8 (2): 105–114. doi:10.1080/13644360304632.
Adams, K. 2010. *Unseen Worlds: Looking through the Lens of Childhood*. London: Jessica Kingsley Publishers.
Adams, K., B. Hyde, and R. Woolley. 2008. *The Spiritual Dimension of Childhood*. London and Philadelphia: Jessica Kingsley Publishers.
Azam, U. 1992. *Dreams in Islam*. Pennsylvania: Dorrance Publishing Co.
Becker, U. 2000. *The Continuum Encyclopedia of Symbols*. New York: Continuum.
Bulkeley, K. 2008. *Dreaming in the World's Religions: A Comparative History*. New York: New York University Press.
Charsley, S. 1973. "Dreams in an Independent African Church'." *Africa* 43: 244–257. doi:10.2307/1158526.
Coles, R. 1990. *The Spiritual Life of Children*. Boston, MA: Peter Davison.
Curley, R. 1992. "Private Dreams and Public Knowledge in Camerounian Independent Church." In *Dreaming, Religion and Society in Africa*, edited by M. C. Jedrej and R. Shaw, 135–152. Leiden: E J Brill.
Dawkins, R. 2017. Science. Accessed 10 October 2018 https://www.richarddawkins.net/
de Souza, M. 2012. "Connectedness and Connectedness: The Dark Side of Spirituality - Implications for Education." *International Journal of Children's Spirituality* 17 (4): 291–303.
Freud, S. 1900/1999. *The Interpretation of Dreams*. Crick, J. (trans.). Oxford: Oxford University Press.

Gadd, A. 2014. Fairy tales and symbols. Accessed 4 January 2019 http://www.anngadd.co.za/2014/12/fairytales-symbols/
Greene, L., and J. Sharman-Burke. 1999. *The Mythic Journey: The Meaning of Myth as a Guide for Life*. London: Eddison Sadd Editions.
Hart, T. 2003. *The Secret Spiritual World of Children*. Maui: Inner Ocean.
Hay, D., and R. Nye. 2006. *The Spirit of the Child*. London and Philadelphia: Jessica Kingsley Publishers.
Hobson, J. A. 1992. *Sleep and Dreams*. North Carolina: Carolina Biological Supply Company.
Hoffman, E. 1992. *Visions of Innocence: Spiritual and Inspirational Experience of Childhood*. Boston, MA: Shambhalla.
Hyde, B. 2008. *Children and Spirituality: Searching for Meaning and Connectedness*. London: Jessica Kingsley.
Jung, C. G. 1936/1969. The collected works of C. G. Jung, Hull, R. F. C; Read, Herbert, Fordham; Adler, Gerhard and McGuire, William, (trans. and eds.), Vol. 9:1, London: Routledge
Lovelock, P., and K. Adams. 2017. "From Darkness to Light: Children Speak of Divine Encounter." *International Journal of Children's Spirituality* 22 (1): 36–48. doi:10.1080/1364436X.2016.1268098.
Maijer, K., S. J. M. C. Palmen, and I. E. C. Sommer. 2017. "Children Seeking Help for Auditory Verbal Hallucinations; Who are They?" *Schizophrenia Research* 183: 31–35. doi:10.1016/j.schres.2016.10.033.
Mental Health Foundation. 2018a. Hallucinations. https://www.mentalhealth.org.uk/a-to-z/h/hallucinations
Mental Health Foundation. 2018b. Hearing voices. https://www.mentalhealth.org.uk/a-to-z/h/hearing-voices
Mind. 2016. How to Cope with Hearing Voices. https://www.mind.org.uk/information-support/types-of-mental-health-problems/hearing-voices/#.W2XAb9HTWhA
New World Encyclopedia. 2015. *Nymph*. Accessed 10 September 2018 http://www.newworldencyclopedia.org/entry/Nymph#Tree
Newcomb, J. 2008. *Angel Kids*. London: Hay House.
Pettersen, A. 2015. "Angels: A Bridge to A Spiritual Pedagogy?" *International Journal of Children's Spirituality* 20: 3–4, 204–217. doi:10.1080/1364436X.2015.1115233.
Potgieter, F., J. L. van der Walt, and C. C. Wolhuter. 2009. "The Divine Dreams of a Sample of South African Children: The Gateway to Their Spirituality." *International Journal of Children's Spirituality* 14 (1): 31–46. doi:10.1080/13644360802658735.
Rankin, M. 2008. *An Introduction to Religious and Spiritual Experience*. London: Continuum.
Rethink Mental Illness. 2016. Hearing Voices. https://www.rethink.org/resources/h/hearing-voices#page2
Robinson, E. 1996. *The Original Vision*. Lampeter: Religious Experience Research Centre.
Sayadmansour, A. 2014. "Neurotheology: The Relationship between Brain and Religion." *Iranian Journal of Neurology* 13 (1): 52–55.
Scott, D. G. 2004. "Retrospective Spiritual Narratives: Exploring Recalled Childhood and Adolescent Spiritual Experiences." *International Journal of Children's Spirituality* 9 (1): 67–79. doi:10.1080/1364436042000200834.
Underhill, J. 1995. *Angels*. Shaftesbury: Element Books .

Living and dying: a window on (Christian) children's spirituality

Elaine Champagne

ABSTRACT
Faith and beliefs about living and dying are fundamental constituents of spiritual development. However, children are seldom asked to talk about their experiences of life and death. This article has a twofold purpose. It first describes children's expressions on living and dying, as heard during a newly developed programme which encourages children's participation as active subjects of their spiritual journey. This programme, the *Grande Halte*, began in 2004 within the changing context of Christian religious education in a secular Québec. Secondly, it proposed a theological reflection informed by the social sciences and the social context of the milieu, and based on children's expressions. It suggests that stories and symbols are needed in order to develop a coherent horizon of meaning in one's life. The relational dimension of the process is also highlighted.

Introduction

Twenty 10-to-12-year-old children were sitting in a large circular tent. The only furniture in the tent was a long and low bench, close to the wall, with a white cloth folded and set to one side. The children had been invited into Jesus' tomb by two adults dressed as the biblical characters Nicodemus and Joseph of Arimathea. A light smell of perfumed oil and incense filled the space. I was sitting among the children, attentive to what was happening. The children's faces showed expectation and curiosity. Another adult, standing among the children, started the conversation: 'Tell me. Does it happen that you ever think about death?' The reaction was quick as lightning and took me by surprise: hands were up, fingers wriggling, bodies moving, children wanting to talk.

The origin of the experience in the tent traces back to 2004, when in the context of Christian faith education, I was asked by the diocese of Saint-Jean-Longueuil from the province of Québec to develop initiatory sessions for children, which would include their life experiences and be supportive of their spiritual journey. The purpose of the programme, entitled the *Grande Halte*, was to engage children in an experiential encounter with the Paschal mystery, that is, the death and resurrection of Christ and its proposed meaning for Christians and any willing human being. The essence of the approach was to have children as active subjects rather than passive objects. This was especially relevant in terms of their concern about living and dying. Because of this specific dynamic, it was clear from the beginning that the role adults would take in the actual setting of the programme would be specific to this process. With the aid of a flexible framework, they would need to journey with the children and facilitate the free expression and growth of their spiritual experience. In French, the adult facilitators received the name *disciples-accompagnateurs*,[1] which reflects the fact that they are not only walking *with* the children in their faith journey, but they are also disciples, also recipients of the children's wisdom, inspired by the Holy Spirit.

In creating the *Grande Halte*, I was supported by a small group of lay ministers and diocesan representatives. They would take up the role of *disciples-accompagnateurs* in the *Grande Halte* and participate in the formation of others. This committee reacted to the development of the content and offered suggestions. When presented with the idea that children would actually talk about life and death, the *disciples-accompagnateurs* were hesitant. Would children be able to explore the questions? How would they react? Would parents approve of the process? An American professor of philosophy, Gareth B. Matthews (1994), had already experienced this type of dialogue with children, as well as the parental resistance to the questions on death and dying. As he points out, '[Parents were] shocked because the very idea of discussing death with children strikes them as offensively inappropriate' (89). However, our programme did not arouse negative reactions, either among children or parents.

The programme started gradually in various parishes and at the end of the summer 2007, a specific formation opportunity was offered to the *disciples-accompagnateurs*, at their request, addressing specifically 'how to talk about death with children'. One of the *disciples-accompagnateurs*' concerns was a lack of information about children's development in understanding death. But it soon became obvious to all that the main resistance came from the discomfort the subject raised for their own adults' spiritual life and journey. To lead this type of conversation with children, the *disciples-accompagnateurs* need to be capable of listening to the questions children raise and to deal with their impact on them, so that they can remain focused on what the children are saying and interact with them in a supportive manner.

Children's active participation in a communicative model of religious education can contribute to its spiritual development (Dillen 2007). But while faith and beliefs about living and dying can be understood as major constituents of spiritual journeys, they are seldom addressed in conversation with children. Except in crisis situations, parents and religious or spiritual educators seldom listen to children's experience and their reflection on life and death. Yet, this need was long highlighted by children themselves (Darcy-Bérubé 1970).

As a result of my involvement in the creation of the programme, my objectives in this article are twofold. First, I introduce the main characteristics of the *Grande Halte* and present children's reactions and expressions when they were given the opportunity to talk about living and dying. In the second part, after a very brief overview of the literature on children and death and dying, I highlight certain socio-cultural issues and initiate a theological reflection on children's worldviews.

Observations

I collected data using a natural observation methodology for three groups of children. I entered into the tent with the children and took some written notes after the end of the meeting. In this first section, I will describe the *Grande Halte* and introduce children's voices.

The political and religious context

Before presenting the *Grande Halte*, it is necessary to address the social, political and religious context in which it was developed. Education in the Québec province of Canada has undergone an accelerated transformation toward a lay configuration at the turn of the 2000s. The confessional status of public elementary and secondary schools was repealed in June 2000. Religious education programmes in schools – Catholic and Protestant – were being modified into a programme of ethics and religious culture, in hope of being more inclusive, both of the broader diversity and of the changing culture of the population. Pastoral and religious animation in schools has been officially replaced since 2001 and 2002, by a service called the Spiritual Support and Community Involvement Service.[2]

Parallel to this process, the main Christian church in Québec, the Catholic Church, not only adapted to this changing social context, but was also involved in a revision of its foundational orientations concerning religious education. In a letter written in 2001, Bishop St-Gelais, then president of the Québec Assembly of Catholic Bishops, indicated some questions needing to be deepened. Those questions included the following two:

- How to change from an approach focused on faith transmission to an approach focused on faith proposal?
- How to promote the experience of meeting with Christ rather than solely teaching truths to transmit?[3]

Beyond the shock wave brought about by these transitions, the various teams involved in formation within dioceses in Québec began to develop various programmes adapted to the specific needs of individuals. While the dioceses and their numerous parishes had, for many years, taken responsibility for sacramental preparation, they now engage in a more global catechetical approach where everyone participates in the human spiritual journey and where Christians are called to witness their hope.[4] The new paradigm reflects a major change in perspective: Christian formation is understood as inscriptive and part of a model of dialogue.

The catechetical context

It is in this context that the diocese of Saint-Jean-Longueuil offers an initiatory programme called the *Grande Halte*, which follows three years of religious education for children, consistent with this orientation. The *Grande Halte* consists of a few meetings with children from nine years of age, for a total duration of about six hours. It is perceived as a road stop, a pause during a pilgrimage or a time of retreat. It is part of an intensive period of preparation prior to the celebration of the sacraments of initiation – Baptism, Confirmation and Eucharist.

The approach used in the *Grande Halte* aims at fostering children's (Christian) spiritual experience. Hence, children are invited to share their experience and to put forth their questions and insights about their life, their values, the challenges they encounter, their hopes and fears, their personal prayer. The process is inductive and initiatory: children are invited to become part of a story, through biblical narratives and through this gestures. The use of symbols is suggestive of meanings born by the Paschal mystery and communicated through the Christian tradition.

The *Grande Halte* considers the children, not only as active subjects but also partners in the approach. It requires hearing their voices, as well as those of their parents or godparents. All freely participate in the programme. It is an attempt to actualise a Church experience of a shared journey, in an effort to deepen faith in Christ. In its process, the *Grande Halte* could also be qualified as liturgical, more performative than explanatory.

The participants

Participants in the first *Grande Halte* included children and parents, the latter sometimes acting as *disciples-accompagnateurs* or volunteers. They were from a suburban area with a wide variety of ethnic and socioeconomic origins. An estimated 4000 children have entered the programme in the last three years (2004–7), approximately 2000 of these in the year 2006/7. The great majority of children were from 9 to 11 years old. An adapted programme for teenagers is under preparation. All the children had previously participated in a three- year religious formation, but the secular environment in which they lived influenced them considerably. I will return to this point later. Parent or adolescent volunteers gathered and prepared the needed material, dressed up, and featured the different biblical characters that the children would encounter during their *pilgrimage*. Adult *disciples-accompagnateurs* led groups of 15 to 40 children. Most of these *disciples-accompagnateurs* were lay ministers, catechists or trainers employed by the diocese. They previously experienced the programme for themselves and received a complementary formation toward it. At least one parent and/ or godparent was invited to participate in the whole programme with each child. On some occasions, they were called upon for a specific contribution.

In the three groups that I witnessed, parents were present and actively participated while also allowing all the space necessary for their child. Approximately a third of these were men. Some mentioned how their child was appreciative of the meetings, singing the theme song everywhere all day long. Among themselves, parents talked about their many commitments, while it was clear that they had chosen to be there and showed no resistance. They also talked with enthusiasm about the coming sacramental celebration.

The course of the programme

It is not the purpose of this article to describe at length the course of the programme. A document in use in the diocese was published, after a few years of experimentation. However, a brief overview may be useful in order to perceive more clearly the context in which the children shared their experience and reflection.

The *Grande Halte* includes four phases. In the first one, the children, after having answered the invitation to join in a pilgrimage toward the celebration of the sacraments of initiation, receive a pilgrim's staff, handcrafted by their parents. On the road, they encounter three characters with whom they dialogue, reflecting about the stories of 'the good things they enjoy in their lives' with the baker, the stories of 'the hard times they experienced and how they were helped out' with the person helped by the Samaritan, and the stories about 'the situations where they took care or took charge with benevolent attitudes toward others' with King David. The road leads the children at the bottom of a wooden cross without body. There, they share prayer.

On their return for the second phase, the group meets with Nicodemus and Joseph of Arimathea. Both men tell the story of what they did at Jesus' death and the sorrow of their loss. They invite the children to follow them into the tomb where they will bury him. At that point, I once heard a child say 'Cool!' with enthusiasm. The children then walk into the vast tent that has been built in the sanctuary, when possible. The parents stay outside. The children in the tent are asked if they ever thought about death. Following the dialogue, a poetical text is heard, from the Paschal Liturgy. The listeners are invited to follow Jesus, who *went down* to awaken all the ones lying in the shadow of death, Adam and Eve, Abraham, Moses, the prophets, and all the ones that preceded us in faith. 'Wake up and rise! Let us leave this place! The feast is ready!' From the outside of the tent, a voice calls every child by his/her name: 'Jonathan, rise up and come out!' A parent welcomes the child and shows a water basin where both silently make the sign of the cross. All can read, printed on the outside of the tent, 'Buried in death with Christ, with Him we will rise from the dead'.

Through the same type of approach, the third and the fourth phases aim to explore the affirmation of the presence of the Holy Spirit and of Christians' witness of the Resurrection in contemporary daily life.

Children's voices

Let us now focus on children's expression of the experience of death in their lives. The comments I present here come from three different groups which experienced the *Grande Halte* during the spring of 2007. As mentioned, I used a process of natural observation to study the three groups. I entered into the tent with the children and took notes only after the end of the meeting. I realise the sample of data is small, and I do not claim that it is representative. However I believe that children's comments can reveal significant insights.

Spontaneity

It was already mentioned that the *Grande Halte* was designed to support children's experience and their expression of it, while presenting them with elements of the Christian faith. A first observation of three such groups points out children's spontaneity and openness to talk about death. In all the groups I have witnessed, children were keen to talk, addressing the *disciple-accompagnateur*, looking at each other, expressing their sadness, their questions, their hope. There was no heaviness during the conversation, but the children were intent in telling their experiences. The *disciple-accompagnateur* simply listened to them, mirroring their words, being present and gently supporting the flow of their conversation.

Sharing experiences

The first comments from one group featured the various losses the children had experienced: grandparents, great-grandparents, a dog, a cat. They said they missed them. A child said she missed her teacher, who was away because she was pregnant. Another mentioned he had lost a friend through betrayal. In a second group, similar comments were heard. A child had a friend whose brother had died. Another had heard about an adult neighbour who was dead.

In a third group, the first child who talked mentioned,

- Death. It makes you think about suffering. Sometimes, some people suffer and they prefer to die.
- You are talking about suicide?
- Yeah …

In that group, many children had relatives or people of their acquaintance who had committed suicide. They named the people they knew. A little later, a child said,

- Jesus, on the cross. He had suffered.

Many talked about suffering. They were sad, with a little nervousness in their gestures and speech. But they did not verbalise their questions or worry more precisely. In the first group, when sadness was expressed, one girl associated it with fear and began to talk about paedophiles and what she had heard on the news. Other children did not follow her lead, but two of them rather expressed their own fears.

The second group mentioned many 'small deaths' they experienced on a more daily basis: feeling alone, being sick, having an arm broken. Free association could then be made with the person helped by the Samaritan they had encountered in the previous meeting.

Recognising universality

When expressing their feelings, a child from the second group said,

- It makes me fearful. I don't think too much about it.

Their uneasiness was observable, but not verbalised.

- We resemble them [the ones who are dead], we are a little like them.
- It will happen to all of us.

The realisation that death is universal and irreversible is part of children's normal cognitive development at that age.

Questioning the destination

In the same group, the conversation continued about where people go when they die. Some of the children's comments were that

- Everyone goes to heaven.
- Some must go the hell because Jesus cannot forgive all the time.
- Some people are forgiven, but they do it again.
- You cannot forgive forty times!
- I think that heaven is for everyone.
- There might be a place while you are waiting.
- Heaven is for everyone. Jesus forgives all the time.

Within their hearts

On many occasions in all groups, children alluded to the fact that they talk to the deceased 'in their hearts'. It was a source of comfort for many. One child half seemed to make fun of it when he said with a smirk, 'They [the deceased] are still there "in our hearts"'. While listening to them, I realised that for most of the children, Jesus was no different from anyone else: One can talk to him 'in his/her heart'. The children may or may not have had the experience of talking with a family member or with Jesus within their hearts. Overall, their comments did not reveal any causal association between Christ's resurrection and the Christian belief that the beloved is alive 'in God'. What they expressed sounded more as obvious fact to them: When someone dies, including Jesus, you can talk to that person in your heart.

Interpretation

What can we draw from these observations? Before entering into a theological reflection based on the children's expressions, it is worthwhile to consider the contributions of the social sciences within the social context of Québec.

Literature on children, death and dying

Literature on children and death and dying is abundant and very diversified. Expertise to support dying children and their grieving siblings is well developed in the health-care milieu (Bluebond-Langner 1978; Sourkes 2002). Children's understanding of death and dying varies according to their developmental level and life experience. Facilitating the expression of their grief by drawing, playing or occasionally by dialogue contributes to their wellbeing. However, it is important that we consider children's awareness about death and dying before they confront the situation in their lives. Children's live are already affected with the deaths of pets or elder relatives as well as other losses bearing the weight of their significance: a blanket, a favourite toy, a pet, a babysitter or a friend, the closeness of a parent, are some examples. But not all adults take seriously children's expressions of loss.

An authentic dialogue, and above all good listening, can support the finding of meaning in children's lives. There is increasing documentation concerning dialogue with children on these issues. 'Children need to learn to mourn and find ways to recover, but the way is not always straight' (Carson 1985, 316). Spiritual support is essential.

Clearly, death is not perceived in the same manner by a toddler and an adolescent: they will not ask the same questions or offer the same meaning. Schonfeld (1993), Busch and Kimble (2001), and Hofer (2004) specify the various concepts involved in children's understanding of biological death, which evolve according to their cognitive development and their life experience, namely, universality, irreversibility, finality (non-functionality), and causality. How a particular child can express his or her perception of death helps us identify the major challenge being faced according to their developmental level. While the understanding of biological death is important, the question of its spiritual relevance for children cannot be dismissed.

Matthews, in his book *The Philosophy of Childhood* (1994), dedicated a whole chapter to a focus on childhood and death. His reflection examines two pieces of children's literature on death that are very well-known to them: *Charlotte's web* and *Tuck everlasting*. His contribution focuses on sick children's development toward the understanding of their own death, while using data from other authors. He does not report the children's conversations.

Stories and fairy tales offer significant support for children in their search for meaning. The theorist Ute Carson pointed out that 'children need suggestions in symbolic form which help transform their inner needs and struggles into thought and action in the outside world' (1985: 317). Following Bettelheim, she invited many groups of children to talk about and then make drawings of various fairy tales involving separation or death. Her article illustrates the use that children make of the many elements of the stories involving attachment, separation and relational reinvestment.

Religious stories can also be supportive of this process. Is it necessary to specify that stories, rather than explanation, bear a significant symbolic power? Symbols and characters with whom one can identify nourish the imagination (Salans, 2004). The children can then reconstruct the story from within, playing with the elements and making sense of them. This process is quite different from the simple affirmation of religious concepts, of which Schonfeld warns: 'Attempts to place religious concepts in concrete terms are usually ineffective and provide little understanding of both physical realities and spiritual beliefs' (1993, 272).

In 1970, within the context of catechetical renewal, Françoise Darcy-Bérubé (1970) studied concepts and attitudes of Canadian children concerning death and beyond. Her aim was to evaluate the impact of religious formation on the children's capability to face the question of death in a healthy manner. At that time, her work was clearly innovative.

More recently, Marcel Hofer (2004) has written a very practical book *Explique-moi la mort… Guide pour accompagner l'enfant en famille et en catéchèse*, addressed to parents and catechists. He describes children's cognitive development and affective needs in regard to the question of death. He also develops a useful chapter on diverse religious perspectives on death and related issues. However, his focus is not on children's voices, but rather on adults' supportive practices, which can facilitate children's grief or grappling with the reality of death, thus helping them in making sense of their loss and finding meaning.

Cultural ethos

The fact that children were so keen in discussing this topic confirms the significance and the value of the time taken to listen to them. Death is omnipresent in games and news, along with the more personal experiences discussed above. Children from 9 to 11 years of age are nearing a more reflective period of their growth, beginning to perceive existential questions without yet naming them. This is exemplified in their dialogue about suffering and about forgiveness.

However, the views expressed in their dialogue are largely influenced by a 'cultural ethos' brought about by conversations they might have heard or participated in, but also by media of all kinds: music, the Internet, movies, books (Harry Potter), and the news are some examples. If Québec was a society of Christendom up until the 1950s, it now has the attributes of a lay society. Christianity, along with other religions and philosophies, is but one voice in the discussion. There is no unanimity in the population regarding the relative importance of that voice. The Commission on reasonable accommodations for immigrants of diverse cultures and religions, held throughout the province, convincingly illustrates this reality (see Gouvernement du Québec 2008).

While being aware of this context, I was surprised when I listened to the children, to realise that for some children, *Jesus was not different from the other deceased. We can talk to him in our hearts*. A new belief had emerged from a cultural practice exterior to a Christian religious coherence. That belief, too, was questioned by at least one child in one group. I would like to clarify what seems to be at stake here.

What happens after death?

In an attempt to offer comfort and support to grieving children, it is common practice to tell them that the deceased is 'present in a different manner', that you can talk to him or her 'in your heart'. On the one hand, while the language about heaven and hell has been deleted for decades from children's books and catechisms, they still discuss it and even mention 'a place while you are waiting'. The transmission of tradition is strong. On the other hand, the idea that one can talk to the deceased within the heart is a common belief, but without any contextual framework. It is presented as fact, a certitude that is not questioned; it is a lay person's affirmation. It is presented as a truth without a story.

When children are told Jesus' story, his death and resurrection, when they hear that one can be relating to him 'in one's heart', nothing can be more factual, nothing can be less surprising. 'Jesus is no different from the other deceased'. Within a Christian perspective, children's understanding seems to be upside-down. There is no point in Jesus' resurrection: When someone dies, you can talk to him or her already.

An a-religious worldview

Jean-Claude Guillebaud offers an interesting reflection on the question of faith and belief in our secularised western societies, which could bring some insight to this observation. In the first part of his book *La force de conviction* (2005), he comments that we have come to dramatic societal changes, which have left us deceived about history and sceptical about the future. The vacuum left by massive rejection of faith has made us more vulnerable to gullibility.

New ideas are more easily believed in as facts, taken for granted. They exist like lonely entities, outside stories, outside the symbolisation of experience, outside the shared communal depths of the human quest expressed in religions, which have endured time. The new worldview is thus eclectic and fragile. The request for openness to the unpredictable, as framed by Erricker (2007), which can be associated with faith, whether one is religious or secular (Welte 1984), falls into nothingness if no foundational coherence can be found or created, when no stories are heard or told. Worse, the new answers fall into the trap of stopping the quest and halting the journey. Rather than being enhanced, spiritual life is impoverished.

Theological interpretation and Christian spirituality

What can be learned from children's words and expressions which can be both significant theologically and nourishing spiritually? The observation opens up many paths. I will choose three which also bear potential implications in faith education. One concerns children's needs, according to what was heard from them. The second mainly concerns adults involved in 'spiritual' dialogue with children. The third appears to concern all of us. It is both a call and a sign of hope.

Stories and history

The children were spontaneous about sharing on death and dying. They were keen in telling their own stories and experiences, open about expressing their fears, willing to reflect together through free associations: 'Jesus on the cross. He has suffered'. They were mature enough to recognise the universality of death, but also to grapple with the question of justice and mercy in an afterlife. They are familiar and mostly comfortable with the view suggesting that they could talk 'within their hearts' with the deceased.

While this view is reassuring to them, it is not questioned, nor it is unfurled in a story, except possibly their own. It is taken for granted, but also disconnected from any belief about what happens to the person who has died: talking to the person within one's heart doesn't say anything about 'where' that person is, or what has become of him or her. Afterlife still remains a question.

I first thought that children would need to ask the question 'why' it is, that we can talk within our hearts. But I realise their need might be even deeper. Not only do they need stories and symbols to make sense of what they experience, but they also need history: the history of a people who shared experiences, questions and a transforming faith through time. They would benefit from religious (Christian) stories and symbols, from an experiential (inner) point of view.

Here again, Guillebaud, and Hauerwas (1981) before him, denounces the rupture with our past, the rejection of our roots, letting our identity become more and more fragile, while preventing us from projecting ourselves into the future. Time is somehow lost along with our history. Children, like all of us, need to discover that history. The questions 'Where do we come from?' and 'Where are we going?' become inseparable from the history of our living faith. The hermeneutical interpretation of our existential quest is indissociable from its collective and historical path.

Come, follow me

I deeply believe that children are not only active subjects of their lives and faith, but also that they can participate in this collective journey of (spiritual) interpretation, if we allow them to do so. In the *Grande Halte*, children were first invited to 'come and see', to follow disciples of Jesus. In doing so, the children enter into the story which adults offer to them. Yet, listening to the children brought us into a different universe than the one we expected or even realised: What does it mean, in a secular world, 'talking in one's heart'? And why is that even possible?

Children's worldview prompts us to different perceptions of the world. Children require that we also follow them. Hence, we are called to an authentic dialogue. How is it that talking in one's heart sounds like praying? Is Jesus really different than our grandparents for that matter? Why is it that we believe that Christ has something to do with what happens to us human beings in the afterlife? If our faith is experienced from within the Christian tradition and is formative of our spiritual lives, how will we 'always be ready to give an explanation to anyone who asks [us] for a reason for [our] hope'? (see 1 Peter 3 :15–16). We need to deepen the realisation that in faith education, we share the learning.

A risen community

In the *Grande Halte*, children are personally called: 'Rise up and come out'. However, their initiatory experience also carries a collective tone. When they come out, a whole community is awaiting them. When formation was given to adult *disciples-accompagnateurs*, they also spontaneously mentioned this communal dimension of resurrection almost as a shocking insight. 'It is the first time that I realise that I am not alone being promised eternal life. It is not only a personal thing. We are many,' said one of them. Being essentially relational, spiritual life – even more the Christian spiritual life – is also about being part of a people.

But there is more. When we enter the historical journey of interpretation shared by Christ's followers and when we allow ourselves to listen to others, including children, we learn from the questions. When we share the learning, we experience from within, and without knowing it, what it is to be a risen community. We experience what we 'proclaim'. The hermeneutical process supports our spiritual experience of the living 'Word'.

Conclusion

In conclusion, it has been noted how uncommon it is in literature that we hear children's words on living and dying. The choice has been made to hear children's experience on the subject during a Christian formation session focused on the Paschal mystery, allowing for their own insights and input. Children's words have then been reinvested as bait for a theological reflection inclusive of their worldview. I deeply believe in the richness that children can bring to our shared spiritual journey. An open window on children's spirituality can lead us to a deeper perspective on our common experience about what it means to be alive and to be called a 'risen people'.

Acknowledgements

A warm thank you to the team members who contributed to making the *Grande Halte* possible, especially to Remi Bourdon, who initiated the whole project. Special thanks also go to Margaret C. Kiely, PhD, *professeur* émérite of the University of Montréal.

Notes

1. In view of the specificity of this term, I will use it throughout the text.
2. See Ministère de l'Éducation du Québec (2000).
3. Mgr Raymond St-Gelais (2001). See also Assemblée des évêques du Québec (2004).
4. 'Always be ready to give an explanation to anyone who asks you for a reason for your hope' (1 Peter 3:15).

References

Assemblée des évêques du Québec. 2004. *Jésus Christ, chemin d'humanisation: Orientations pour la formation à la vie chrétienne* [Jesus Christ, the path of humanisation: Guidelines for training in Christian life]. Montréal: Médiaspaul.
Bluebond-Langner, M. 1978. *The private world of dying children.* Princeton, NJ: Princeton University Press.
Busch, T., and C. Kimble. 2001. Grieving children: Are we meeting the challenge? *Pediatric Nursing* 27, no. 4: 414–18.
Carson, U. 1985. Teachable moments occasioned by 'small deaths'. *Issues in Comprehensive Pediatric Nursing* 8, no. 1/6: 315–43.
Darcy-Bérubé, F. 1970. Concepts et attitudes concernant la mort et l'au-delà. Une recherché théoritique, exploratoire et expérimentale chez un groupe d'enfants canadiens catholiques [Concepts and attitudes about death and beyond. Theoretical research, exploration and experiment in a group of Catholic Canadian children]. PhD thesis, Religious Studies, University of Ottawa, Ottawa, ON, Canada.
Dillen, A. 2007. Religious participation of children as active subjects: Toward a hermeneutical- communicative model of religious education in families with young children. *International Journal of Children's Spirituality* 12, no. 1: 37–49.
Erricker, C. 2007. Children's spirituality and postmodern faith. *International Journal of Children's Spirituality* 12, no. 1: 51–60.
Gouvernement du Québec. 2008. Commission de consultation sur les practiques d'accomodement reliées aux différences culturelles [Commission consultation on accommodation related to cultural differences]. http://www.accommodements.qc.ca/index-en.html (accessed June 25, 2008).
Guillebaud, J.-C. 2005. *La force de conviction. A quoi pouvons-nous croire?* [The strength of conviction. What can we believe?]. Paris: Seuil.
Hauerwas, S. 1981. *A community of character: Toward a constructive Christian social ethic* Notre Dame, IN: Notre Dame University Press.
Hofer, M. 2004. *Explique-moi la mort ... Guide pour accompagner l'enfant en famille et en catéchèse.* Pédagogie catéchètique 16. Brussels: Lumen Vitae.
Matthews, G. 1994. *The philosophy of childhood.* Cambridge, Harvard University Press.

Ministère de l'Éducation du Québec. 2000. *Responding to the diversity of moral and religious expectations,* Québec: Ministère de l'Éducation du Québec.
Salans, M. 2004. *Storytelling with children in crisis.* London: Jessica Kingsley.
Sourkes, B. 2002. *Armfuls of time: The psychological experience of the child with a life-threatening illness.* Pittsburgh, PA: University of Pittsburgh Press.
Schonfeld, D. 1993. Talking with children about death. *Journal of Pediatric Health Care* 7, no. 6: 269–74.
St-Gelais, R. 2001. La catéchèse: une vision commune. Assemblée des évêques catholiques du Québec website. http//:www.eveques.qc.ca/documents/2001/20011024f.html (accessed December 6, 2007).
Welte, B. 1984. *Qu'est-ce que croire?* [What is believing?]. Héritage et projet 28. Montréal: Fides.

How do Finnish pre-adolescents perceive religion and spirituality?

Martin Ubani and Kirsi Tirri

ABSTRACT
The purpose of this study is to investigate how Finnish pre-adolescents perceive religion and spirituality. The participants of the study are 12- to 13-year-old Grade 6 pupils (*N* = 102). The pupils were asked to give their meanings of religion and spirituality. The data includes over 700 written expressions on the two concepts. The qualitative content analysis of the data produced three dimensions. They were called the institutional dimension, the humanistic dimension, and the supernatural dimension. The students emphasized different dimensions in the data concerning religion compared to the data concerning spirituality. Most of the meanings given to religion belonged to the institutional dimension (68.2%). In the data concerning spirituality most of the meanings belonged to the humanistic dimension (66.2%).

Introduction

The purpose of this study is to investigate the meanings given to the concepts of religion and spirituality by Finnish Grade 6 students (*N* = 102). The majority of studies concerning the relationship between religion and spirituality have been philosophical or theoretical in nature and empirical approaches have been rare. Our aim is to provide some empirical data that would enrich the discussion concerning religion and spirituality. In this paper, we present some results of our ongoing research project on spirituality of different age groups (Tirri, 2004). The data discussed in this paper involves written opinions of Grade 6 students (12- to 13-year-olds). The data includes over 700 written opinions on the concepts of religion and spirituality. The concrete research questions of this study are:

1. What meanings do Finnish Grade 6 students give to the concepts of religion and spirituality?
2. What is the difference between their perceptions of the two concepts?

This study is part of a larger project led by Professor Kirsi Tirri called Actualizing Finnish Giftedness, funded by Finnish Academy. The project has investigated the spirituality of different populations. For instance, the Grade 6 students in this study have participated in a number of studies. In addition to completing the DIT test measuring moral reasoning, they have completed the Multiple Intelligence Questionnaire extended with a test of spiritual sensitivity (Tirri *et al.*, 2006). There have also been qualitative studies focusing on the relational aspect in the spirituality of girls (Tirri & Ubani, 2005), and on science and nature as a source of spirituality for the gifted boys (Ubani, 2006a). In addition, there has been one phenomenological study exploring the nature of their spiritual experiences (Ubani, 2006b).

Religion and spirituality

The meanings given to the concepts of religion and spirituality have evolved over the centuries. William James (2003) defined religion as 'the feelings, acts and experiences of individual men in their solitude' (p. 32). Since the time of James, few psychologists have taken a serious look at religious institutions and the roles they play in shaping character. Today some writers use the terms religion and spirituality interchangeably to add linguistic variety to their terminology. However, many researchers use a contrast with spirituality to define religion. In these definitions religion is usually defined as the organizational, the ritual and the ideological. The spiritual then refers to the personal, the affective, the experiential and the thoughtful. The reminder that an individual can be spiritual without being religious or religious without being spiritual has become a standard part of many papers on spirituality (Pargament, 1999). The European view emphasizes people's search for meaning in relation to big existential questions as important part of spirituality (Stifoss-Hanssen, 1999). In the multicultural world spirituality can be expressed not only by very religious people but by atheists and agnostics, by people deeply engaged in ecology and other idealistic endeavours, and by people inspired by religious impulses not easily understood by classic religious concepts (e.g. sacredness). According to this view spirituality must be seen as a wider concept than religion. This kind of understanding of these concepts indicates that religion and spirituality share some common areas but they also have their own areas of interests (Stifoss-Hanssen, 1999).

The difference in connotations of 'religion' and 'spirituality' has been empirically studied, too. Zinnbauer *et al.* (1997) have reported on the differences on perceptions concerning 'religiousness' and 'spirituality' in the US. The participants ($N = 346$) of the study were from different religious backgrounds and aged between 15- to 85-years. The research concluded that religiousness and spirituality share similar connotations but have also differences in content. 'Religiousness' referred to organized activities, performance of rituals as well as commitment to organizational or institutional activities or dogma. As a contrast, 'spirituality' included references to humane behaviour in daily life, including integrating one's values and beliefs into daily life (p. 557). In the study of Zinnbauer *et al.*, the transcendental quality of reality and belief in a higher power of some kind was the overlapping quality in religiousness and spirituality.

Religion and spirituality in Finnish school education

In many countries all over the world, the school curriculum should be one that promotes the spiritual, moral, cultural, mental, and physical development of students. Furthermore, education should prepare students for the opportunities, responsibilities, and experiences of adult life (Best, 2000; SCAA, 1996). For example, in Finland the goal of elementary education is to support the development of the whole person of the students, rather than merely the cognitive domain (National Core Curriculum for Basic

Education, 2004). This kind of education acknowledges the importance of the social and affective domains in students' development including their spiritual and religious concerns. The nature and relationships of spiritual and religious education has been very much debated in the educational international journals (Blake, 1996; Lewis, 2000; Pridmore, 2002). According to Carr (1995), the easiest solution to the problem of the curricular accommodation of spiritual development is to view spiritual education as simply one aspect or dimension of the general business of religious education. The problem with this approach, however, is that spiritual development would be available only to those who belong to and participate in some form or other of religious faith. Furthermore, the school curriculum has many other subjects besides religious education with considerable potential for the development of spiritual qualities—art, history, literature, the study of nature and mathematics (Carr, 1995).

According to Lewis (2000) children bring with them a spiritual aspect or sensibil-ity. The school may wish to develop and enrich this sensibility, or it may wish to ignore it. Ignorance of spirituality will still lead to learning in this area, for instance this aspect of one's being is unimportant or inferior to purely cognitive ways of understanding (Lewis, 2000). David Hay suggests that in the secularized society children learn not to discuss spiritual issues openly (Hay, 1998). However, many researchers view spiritual awareness as a universal human attribute. Robert Coles has had numerous conversations with children from different countries and cultural backgrounds and he thinks it is a mistake to give priority to intellectual operations in our attempts to understand children's spirituality (Coles, 1990). Spirituality can be defined as 'awareness that there is something greater than the course of everyday events'. In children's lives events such as birth, death, sadness, love, joy and special occasions are related to this definition. Furthermore, activities such as painting, drawing, sorting, matching, plays, stories and singing can make room for spiritual awareness (Hay, 1998). Lewis (2000) defines spiritual education as the cultivation of important qualities of the heart and the mind. This task is not seen as the preserve of religious education, moral education, the arts, or any other area of the curriculum in isolation. We are all searching for meaning and a sense of identity.

In Finland we provide compulsory religious education in schools. Traditionally, religious education has been the most debated subject in the Finnish curriculum for comprehensive schools. The role of the Lutheran church and its doctrine on religious education in schools has been questioned. In addition, the significance of the Christian heritage in Finnish culture and education has been constantly discussed. (Puolimatka & Tirri, 2000). About 84% of the Finnish population belongs to the Lutheran church but the trend is rapidly decreasing. This is increasingly true in the urban areas. For instance, in 2005 in Helsinki only 69% of the population belonged to the Lutheran church. However, instead of becoming members in another religious tradition, more and more people choose to stay unaffiliated. Hence, the largest religious minority is the Finnish–Greek Orthodox Church with less than 60,000 members. However, recent studies show that between the years 1981 and 2000 the percentage of Finnish people who believe in God, Spirit or some kind of life force has increased from 71% to 80% (Niemelä, 2003, p. 202).

At the primary level one hour of religious education is given to the pupils each week. The content of religious education at the primary level depends on the religious affiliation of the student. Despite of the decline in Lutheran church membership, in 2004 about 95% of the students took Lutheran RE. Teaching at the secondary level is divided into periods. The students have one compulsory course and may then choose additional courses. The courses include world religions, ethics, church history and Lutheran dogmatics.

In 2004, the National Core Curriculum for Basic Education (NCCBE, 2004) replaced the previous guidelines (NCCBE, 1994) for primary school. It stated the objectives and requirements for primary education as well as for each subject, including religious education. In the Finnish school education spirituality is integrated into religious education. The national curriculum in 2004 states that the general objective in RE is to approach 'life's religious and ethical dimensions … from the standpoint of the pupil's own growth, and as a broader social phenomenon' (NCCBE, 2004, p. 202). Religious education is considered to be the main source for developing spirituality. This is illustrated explicitly in the following sub-aims of religious education. The aim of the instruction is:

> … to familiarize the pupil with his or her own religion, familiarize the pupil with the Finnish spiritual tradition, introduce the pupil to other religions, help the pupil understand the cultural and human meaning of religions, and to educate the pupil in ethical living and help him or her understand the ethical dimension of religion. (NCCBE, 2004, p. 202)

However, the use of the term spirituality is problematic in Finland. For instance, the concept 'spiritual' is found only once and only in the official English translation. The exact English translation of the 'spiritual tradition' is actually 'religious heritage'. This reflects the recent debate concerning the nature of RE in Finland. There have been efforts to distinguish between religious instruction and religious practice. The translation seems to reveal a bias and a will to attribute spiritual life solely to religion and especially to Lutheranism.

Erricker (2000, p.18) has identified three central questions concerning the primary responsibilities of religious education. Firstly, there is the question whether RE is about investigating the concepts and concerns intrinsic to religious belief, such as God and the transcendent. Secondly, clarification is needed for whether RE is about understanding the diverse forms that religion takes. This is primarily constituted by a study of 'world religions'. The third question is whether RE is about understanding different value systems and, primarily about enabling the pupils to develop their own. Generally, the objectives of NCCBE 2004 focus on the development of the individual's own views. The other aims serve this objective. The study of world religions and understanding different value systems are subject to the pupil's development. For instance, Kallioniemi (2004, p.150) has pointed out that RE in Finnish education emphasizes 'learning from' and 'learning about' religion. Furthermore, Puolimatka and Tirri (2000) have found common ground between the Finnish religious education and what Nel Noddings (1993) calls educating intelligent belief. The Finnish religious education system acknowledges the need for enhancing children's critical capacities for evaluating their own confession and the development of their understanding of the contextuality of religious truth claims. It is believed that the pedagogical interpretation of confessionality can develop the individual's own views and beliefs. In practice, religious education in Finnish schools starts with a familiar religious context. (Puolimatka & Tirri, 2000). A sufficient knowledge of one tradition helps to understand the other belief systems.

Data and methods

Participants

A total of 101 Grade 6 students (12- to 13-years-old) participated in the study. These pupils attend a special school in Helsinki, Finland, which includes Grades 3 to the upper secondary school. The school has its own special curriculum and applicants for Grade 3 are tested with entrance examination containing linguistic, logical and spatial tasks. The study included all four Grade 6 classes. Of the students participating, 60 were girls and 41 were boys.

Instrumentation

The data was collected in autumn 2003. It was gathered with a brainstorming task presented in the handbook of religious education (Hammond *et al.*, 1990, p. 7). The students formed 20 mixed groups with five students in each group. The students were given the following instruction:

1. Take a large sheet of paper and write the word RELIGION in the middle. Appoint someone to write down ideas. For the next five minutes, the members of the group should call out as many associations with the word 'Religion' as they can think of. Everything must be recorded. There should be no discussion or censorship of ideas. All ideas should be respected!
2. Repeat the exercise on another sheet of paper, this time with the word SPIRITUALITY.

The students produced a total of 475 expressions concerning religion, and 305 concerning spirituality. The meanings given to both concepts were further analysed with inductive content analysis (Bos & Tarnai, 1999, p. 662). The expressions were grouped according to their different meanings. They formed 11 sub-categories. All the sub-categories could be collected under three main dimensions. The expressions in *the institutional dimension* referred to the established and specialized forms of religious and spiritual life. The meanings in *the supernatural dimension* referred to transcendental religious and spiritual phenomena. The expressions in the *humanistic dimension* included issues related to all aspects of human life.

The authors acted as autonomous readers who both rated the expressions independently of each other. The inter-rater reliability was 0.96, based on the independent scoring of 25 expressions in both religion and spirituality by two raters and an index calculated by the formula (number of rater agreement)/(number of expressions). The data that was rated represented 10% of the different expressions in all the data.

Students' perceptions of religion and spirituality

The most common expressions

The students gave more expressions for religion ($N=475$) than spirituality ($N=305$). The left column in Table 1 lists the 10 most common expressions that were given for religion.

The most common expressions concerning religion were typically connected to Christianity. Generally, among the most common expressions there were more meanings that referred to the Roman Catholic tradition than to the Evangelic– Lutheran church. The most common expression concerning religion was 'church'. It was mentioned 15 times. In Finnish culture 'church' epitomizes religion. It is also an essential concept in the Lutheran tradition. It is used as a reference to the communion of saints. In addition, the church building is the usual setting for religious activities. 'Jesus' ($N=14$) and 'God' ($N=13$) were mentioned almost as often as 'church'. Especially in a Nordic context Jesus and God are the two central figures in religion. Moreover, the Lutheran RE at the primary level concentrates on God and Jesus (NCCBE, 2004, p. 203). The fourth most usual expressions were 'Bible' ($N=12$) and 'Pope' ($N=12$). The 'cross' was the sixth most usual expression concerning religion. The students mentioned it ten times. The Bible, the Pope and the cross are the main symbols of Christianity. For instance, the Bible is the holy book of Christianity and the slogan of Reformation, 'Sola scriptura', proclaims its authority. The Pope is among the most influential religious and political leaders in the world and his activities are also covered intensively by the Finnish media. The cross is visible in the everyday life of the students. For instance, it is used in jewellery and is also represented in the Finnish flag. The next most common expressions attributed to religion were given eight times. They were 'Roman Catholic', 'Martin Luther', 'Reformation' and 'RE teacher'. This reflects the fact that during Grade 6 the students are introduced to the history of the Reformation and the rift between Protestantism and the Pope. As a conclusion, pupils seem to attribute to 'religion' the themes that are currently taught in RE classes.

Table 1. The 10 most common expressions concerning religion and spirituality

Religion	(N = 475)	Spirituality	(N = 305)
Church	15	Spirit	9
Jesus	14	Spiral	8
God	13	Spirit–movie	7
Bible	12	Devotional life	5
Pope	12	Yoga	5
Cross	10	Latin word	4
Roman catholic	8	Rituals	4
Martin Luther	8	Spiritual world	4
Reformation	8	Spiritism	4
RE teacher	8	Strange word	4

The right column in Table 1 lists the 10 most common expressions concerning spirituality. They were words that were all derived from the Latin word *spiritualitas* that refers to all aspects of life that is somehow connected with the spirit of God. Usually the expressions concerning spirituality were not exclusively connected to Christianity. This was an essential difference between the most common expressions concerning spirituality and religion. The expression that was mentioned most often in the data concerning spirituality was 'spirit'. The students mentioned it nine times. The second most usual expression that was attributed to spirituality was 'spiral' ($N = 8$) and the third most common was the movie 'Spirit' ($N = 7$). Evidently this expression referred to a Disney movie showing at that time which features a horse called 'Spirit'. The fourth most frequent expressions were 'yoga' (N = 5) and 'devotional life' (N = 5). The fifth most common expressions were mentioned four times each. They were 'rituals', 'spiritism', 'Latin word', 'spiritual word', and 'strange word'. It is possible that 'rituals', 'spiritism' and even 'spiritual world' refer to mystical practices. Finally, the pupils gave the meanings such as 'Latin word' and 'strange word' to spirituality. This finding echoes the views of Stifoss-Hanssen (1999) that in a Nordic context the word 'spirituality' is not part of everyday language.

The three dimensions

General overview of the dimensions

The students gave more expressions concerning religion (N = 475) than spirituality (N = 305). The analysis of the data produced three dimensions (Figure 1). The left bars in Figure 1 show the amount of meanings given to religion and the right bars show the amount of meanings given to spirituality. The largest category was named *the institutional dimension*, because all the expressions in this category referred to different kinds of established and specialized forms of religious and spiritual life. The majority of the expressions (N = 324) in this dimension were given to religion. The minority of the expressions in this dimension were given to spirituality (N = 54).

The second largest category was named *the humanistic dimension*. The expressions in this category referred to different aspects of human life and culture. The majority of the expressions in this dimension (N = 202) were given to spirituality while the minority were given to religion (N = 109). The difference in emphasis between religion and spirituality echoes previous studies. According to earlier studies, religion is widely portrayed as institutional and formal while spirituality is described as 'the personal, the

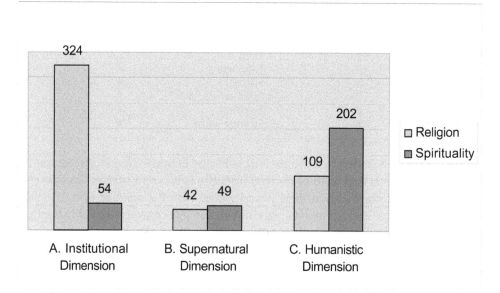

Figure 1. Three dimensions of religion and spirituality.

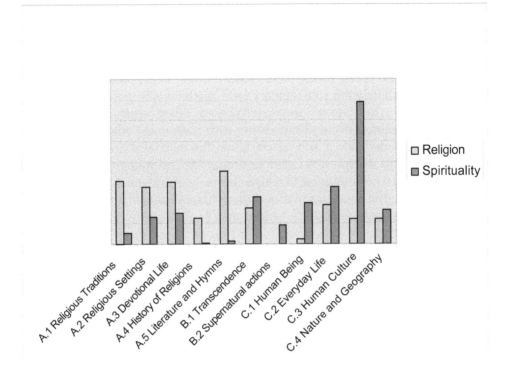

Figure 2. The distribution of the meanings in the three dimensions.

affective, the experiential, and the thoughtful' (Hay, 1998; Pargament, 1999). In other words, religion is distant and organized while spirituality is humane. The smallest category was called *the supernatural dimension*. It consisted of meanings that referred to transcendental religious and spiritual phenomena. In this dimension the number of expressions given to spirituality (*N*=49) and religion (*N*=42) were very even. The small percentage of meanings belonging to the supernatural dimension may reflect the fact that in a predominantly Lutheran context the supernatural phenomena belong more to the sphere of sci-fi than to religion or mainstream spirituality.

The institutional dimension

The students emphasized different aspects of life in the data concerning religion than in the data concerning spirituality. The meanings that were given to religion belonged most typically to the institutional dimension (68.2%). This was in clear contrast to the number of meanings given to spirituality that belonged to the institutional dimension (17.7%).

Figure 2 shows the distribution of meanings given to religion and spirituality in the eleven sub-categories. The left bars show the distribution of all the meanings given to religion and the right bars show the distribution of the meanings given to spirituality. The institutional dimension included five sub-categories (A1–A5). They were called *religious traditions, religious settings, devotional life, history of religions,* and *literature and hymns* (Figure 2). In the institutional dimension the meanings given to religion focused on Christianity and other world religions while the meanings given to spirituality emphasized new religious movements and world religions other than Christianity. The largest sub-category in the data concerning religion, *literature and hymns*, belonged to the institutional dimension. The meanings given to religion in this sub-category focused on incidents and characters in the Bible. The only expressions that the students gave to spirituality in this sub-category were 'myths' and 'legends'. The second largest sub-category in the data concerning religion was called *religious traditions*. The meanings given to religion included expressions such as 'Roman Catholic' and 'Islam' while spirituality included 'Wicca' and 'Hare Krishna'. The third largest sub-category in the meanings given to religion was called *devotional life*. The students gave religion meanings that focused on communal Christian observances and rituals as well as individual devotional life. The meanings that were given to spirituality in this sub-category did not refer to Christianity exclusively. Instead they emphasized 'yoga' and rituals in general.

The meanings that belonged to the fourth largest sub-category in the institutional dimension were called *religious settings*. In the data concerning religion, the meanings focused on religious professionals and had a Christian emphasis. While in this sub-category the students gave to religion meanings such as 'monk', 'priest' and 'pope', the meanings given to spirituality expressions such as 'fakir' and 'mediums'. The fifth sub-category in the institutional dimension was called *history of religions*. The data concerning religion included meanings such as 'Reformation' and 'Crusades'. The only meaning that belonged to this sub-category in the meanings that were given to spirituality was 'witch-hunts'.

The supernatural dimension

In the study by Zinnbauer *et al.* (1997), the transcendental quality of reality and belief in a higher power was the overlapping quality in religiousness and spirituality (ibid.). Likewise, the meanings given by pre-adolescents to 'religion' and 'spirituality' included a supernatural dimension. However, the preadolescents of this study did not put much emphasis on the supernatural aspect of religion and spirituality.

The supernatural dimension included 16.1% of the meanings given to spirituality and 8.8% of the expressions given to religion. This dimension included various meanings that focused on the transcendental realm. The supernatural dimension had two sub-categories (B1–B2). The sub-categories were called *transcendence* and *supernatural actions*. The sub-category called supernatural actions referred to phenomena that exceed the ordinary everyday life. In this category the students gave to spirituality meanings such as 'raising spirits' or 'exorcism'. There were no meanings given to religion that belonged to this sub-category. The other sub-category in this dimension was called *transcendence* because it referred to supernatural reality and creatures. In the meanings given to religion, meanings such as 'God', 'Allah' and 'angels' belonged to this sub-category. The meanings given to spirituality in the sub-category called transcendence focused more on different kinds of spirits and evil beings such as 'Satan' and the 'devil'.

The humanistic dimension

The humanistic dimension was the third category. It included meanings concerning different aspects of human life and culture. Most of the meanings that were given to spirituality belonged to this dimension (66.2%). This dimension was less frequent in the data concerning religion (22.9%). In the data the humanistic dimension consisted of subcategories C1–C4 which are called *human being, everyday life, human culture,* and *nature and geography*.

The largest sub-category in the data concerning spirituality (34.4%) belonged to the humanistic dimension. This sub-category was called *human culture*. The meanings given to spirituality that belonged to this sub-category focused on art and literature while the meanings that were given to religion also had expressions referring to conflicts such as the war in Iraq and the destruction of the World Trade Center. The sub-category called *everyday life* was the second largest sub-category in the meanings given to spirituality. The content of this sub-category was similar for the data concerning religion and for the expressions given to spirituality. The meanings in this sub-category referred mostly to the students' school lives, food and items such as candles. The third largest sub-category in the meanings given to spirituality was called *human being*. This sub-category was also quite similar in the data concerning religion and spirituality. It referred to human psychology and physiology. However, the meanings given to spirituality included expressions focusing on the inner life of the individual, such as 'concentration' and 'contemplation' that were absent in the meanings given to religion. The last sub-category in the humanistic dimension was called *nature and geography*. In this sub-category the differences in the meanings given to religion and spirituality focused on geography. The students gave meanings to religion that referred to Middle East while the expressions given to spirituality emphasized Asia.

Concluding remarks

In this study, the meanings that the students gave to religion and spirituality were overlapping. The analysis revealed three dimensions in the meanings that the students gave to religion and spirituality. They were called the institutional dimension, the supernatural dimension and the humanistic dimension. *The institutional dimension* refers to the established and specialized forms of religious and spiritual life. The meanings in *the supernatural dimension* refer to transcendental phenomena. *The humanistic dimension* focuses on issues that are related to different aspects of human life. The institutional dimension, the supernatural dimension, and the humanistic dimension' provide a comprehensive framework for comparative studies concerning the topic.

The students emphasized different dimensions in the data concerning religion than in the data concerning spirituality. In this study, most of the meanings that the students gave to religion belonged to the institutional dimension (68.2%). The meanings given to religion often referred to Christianity and other world religions. Religious settings, professionals and devotional life are thought to be an integral part of religion. The pupils attributed to 'religion' the themes that are currently taught in RE classes. The Grade 6 emphasis on Martin Luther and Reformation was present in the data as there were many expressions referring also to the Roman Catholic Church and Pope. The study implies that the RE provides wide and general knowledge about the phenomenon of religion.

In the data concerning spirituality most of the meanings belonged to the humanistic dimension (66.2%). The expressions concerning spirituality were often connected to new religious movements and world religions. In Grade 6, the core content of the curriculum of the Lutheran RE includes familiarizing 'in general terms' with world religions and the main features of religious lives connected to them (NCCBE, 2004, 205). Generally in school books, Christianity is often illustrated with pictures of churches, the Pope and symbols. The pictures of other religions and especially the eastern traditions emphasize the spiritual side more, such as rituals, incense, and prayer. As different religions include similar elements, the difference of emphasis is most evident in the wording that explains the content of the picture. Deconstructing the explanations of the pictures that are presented in the school books would probably show a bias attributing humanity, depth, and the spiritual aspect to eastern traditions and the distant and an institutional aspect to western Christianity. However, a proper introduction to different traditions should aim at presenting the institutional, the supernatural and the humane aspects equally and fairly.

In Finland, religious education is given according to the religious denominations of the students. In most cases the denomination is Lutheran. The Finnish curriculum does not explicitly use the word spirituality. The concept is found only once and only in the English translation. The actual wording that is translated in English as 'spiritual' is in Finnish 'religious' (NCCBE, 2004, p. 202). However, nowadays labeling the inner life of the pupil as 'religious' is problematic. Generally, there should be more discussion about what is the actual spiritual tradition or religious heritage of the pupil. The replacement of 'religion' with 'spirituality' in the curriculum implies that the Finnish education policy lacks conceptual clarity and/or assumes homogenous beliefs and values among children. Clive Erricker (2000, p. 58) claims that spiritual education must go beyond religious education for it to embrace young people and the plurality of cultural experiences and values. It should be added that the Finnish religious education must go beyond the *religious* to embrace the *spiritual* in the pupil. If religious education, of all subjects, does not use 'spirituality' explicitly in the curriculum, then why not substitute the subject with literature, history or cultural education? Finnish education cannot properly address the spiritual in pupils if the school does not become conscious of spiritual development as an explicit educational aim. Education should try to find ways to integrate religion and spirituality as well as to maintain the distance between the two phenomena.

Research has shown that during puberty attitudes toward religion become more critical and negative (Tamminen, 1991). At the same time the pre-adolescents are approaching the age when the struggle concerning the sense of significance and purpose is probably the most intense in their lives (Fry, 1998, p. 91; Tirri et al., 2005). In other words, their spiritual life is active, while the religious life may not be. In order to make religious education relevant and motivating for the pupils, their critical attitudes and search for meaning should be seen as an asset in the classroom. Noddings (1993, p. 2) claims that serious treatment of existential questions can contribute not only to the spiritual growth of children but to their intellectual, moral, and emotional development as well. Education of the whole person is not based on segregation of different aspects of human life. Instead, it seeks to develop different abilities such as moral, spiritual, social and cultural qualities comprehensively along with the student's cognitive skills (Best, 2000). The holistic approach to education should encourage the students to find the spiritual in religion as well as the religion in spirituality. The task used in this study integrates the cognitive with the spiritual and social domains by guiding the pupils to work together and analyse religion and spirituality. In a pluralistic world it is important to study how different populations perceive religion and spirituality. Religious and spiritual education should provide children with tools for analysing religion and spirituality as universal and parallel forms of human behaviour. When we are teaching, we should acknowledge that the concepts 'religion' and 'spirituality' mean different things to different people. If education is to promote intelligent belief (Noddings, 1993), it should explore the connotations of these concepts and critically evaluate the meaning they convey to our beliefs and attitudes.

References

Best, R. (Ed.) (2000) *Education for spiritual, moral, social and cultural development* (London, Continuum).
Blake, N. (1996) Against spiritual education, *Oxford Review of Education*, 22, 443–456.
Bos, W. & Tarnai, C. (1999) Content analysis in empirical social research, *International Journal of Educational Research*, 31, 659–671.
Carr, D. (1995) Towards a distinctive conception of spiritual education, *Oxford Review of Education*, 21, 83–98.
Coles, R. (1990) *The spiritual life of children* (Boston, Houghton-Mifflin).
Erricker, C. (2000) A critical review of religious education, in: C. Erricker, & J. Erricker *Reconstructing religious, spiritual and moral education* (London, RoutledgeFalmer), 15–35.
Emmons, R. A. & Crumpler, C. A. (1999) Religion and spirituality? The roles of sanctification and the concept of God, *International Journal for the Psychology of Religion*, 9, 17–24.
Fry, P. S. (1998) The development of personal meaning and wisdom in adolescence: a re-examination of moderating and consolidating factors and influences, in: T. P. Wong & P. S. Fry (Eds) *The human quest for meaning. A handbook of psychological research and clinical applications* (Mahwah, Lawrence Erlbaum), 91–110.
Hammond, J., Hay, D., Moxon, J., Netto, B., Straugheir, G. & Williams, C. (1990) *New methods in RE teaching: an experiental approach* (London, Oliver & Boyd).
Hay, D. (1998) *The spirit of the child* (London, HarperCollins).
James, W. (2003) *The varieties of religious experience* (New York, Signet Classic). (Original work published 1902.)
Kallioniemi, A. (2004) Research in religious education in Finland, in: R. Larsson & C. Gustavsson (Eds) *Towards a European perspective on religious education* (University of Lund, Bibliotheca Theologiae Practicae 74), 145–156.
Lewis, J. (2000) Spiritual education as the cultivation of qualities of the heart and mind. A reply to Blake and Carr, *Oxford Review of Education*, 26, 263–283.
National Core Curriculum for Basic Education (1994) (Helsinki, Finnish National Board of Education).
National Core Curriculum for Basic Education (2004) (Helsinki, Finnish National Board of Education).
Niemelä, K. (2003) Uskonnollisuus eri väestöryhmissä [Religiousness of different age groups], in: K. Kääriäinen, K. Niemelä & K. Ketola (Eds) *Moderni kirkkokansa* [Modern Church People] *Suomalaisten uskonnollisuus uudella vuosituhannella* (Kirkon tutkimuskeskuksen julkaisuja 82), 187–220.
Noddings, N. (1993) *Educating for intelligent belief of unbelief* (New York, Teacher's College).
Pargament, K. I. (1999) The psychology of religion and spirituality? Yes and no, *International Journal for the Psychology of Religion*, 9, 3–16.
Pridmore, J. (2002) Talking of God and Talking of Fairies: discourses of spiritual development in the works of George MacDonald and in the curriculum, *International Journal of Children's Spirituality*, 7, 23–35.
Puolimatka, T & Tirri, K. (2000) Religious education in Finland: promoting intelligent belief? *British Journal of Religious Education*, 23, 38–44.

Rodger, A. (2000) Moral, spiritual, religious—are they synonymous?, in: M. Leicester, C. Modgil & S. Modgil (Eds) *Education, culture and values. Volume 5: spiritual and religious education* (London, Falmer), 3–14.

School Curriculum and Assessment Authority (SCAA) (1996) *Education for adult life: the spiritual and moral development of young people.* Discussion paper No. 6 (London, SCAA).

Stifoss-Hanssen, H. (1999) Religion and spirituality: what a European ear hears, *International Journal for the Psychology of Religion,* 9, 25–33.

Tamminen, K. (1991) *Religious development in childhood and youth.* Annales academiae scientarium Fenniae. Ser. B/259 (Helsinki, Federation of Finnish Scientific Societies).

Tirri, K. (2004) Spirituality in religious education, in: R. Larsson & C. Gustavsson (Eds) *Towards a European perspective on religious education* (University of Lund, Bibliotheca Theologiae Practicae 74), 344–352.

Tirri, K. & Ubani, M. (2005) How do gifted girls perceive the meaning of life? *Gifted Education International,* 19, 266–274.

Tirri, K., Nokelainen, P., Ubani, M. (2006) Conceptual definition and empirical validation of the spiritual sensitivity scale, *Journal of Empirical Theology,* 19, 37–62.

Tirri, K., Tallent-Runnels, M. & Nokelainen, P. (2005) A cross-cultural study of pre-adolescents' moral, religious and spiritual questions, *British Journal of Religious Education,* 27, 207–214.

Ubani, M. (2006a) Male, science, giftedness ... and spirituality? A report of an empirical study of Finnish pre-adolescent boys, paper presented at the *American Educational Research Association Conference,* San Fransisco.

Ubani, M. (2006b) What makes life spiritual? in: K. Tirri (Ed.) *Religion, spirituality and identity* (Bern, Peter Lang).

Zinnbauer, B., Pargament, K. I., Cole, B., Rye, M., Butter, E., Belavich, T., Hipp, K., Scott, A. & Kadar, J. (1997) Religion and spirituality: unfuzzying the fuzzy, *Journal for the Scientific Study of Religion,* 36, 549–564.

The personae of the spiritual child: taking pictures of the heart using technology and tablets

Kathleen Harris

ABSTRACT
What does the spiritual child look like? The spiritual child begins life exploring the world, learning through sensory experiences and new discoveries. A protagonist and a collaborator, the spiritual child is a communicator who engages in social interactions, constructing his or her own learning, curious about the world. The purpose of this article is to explore several personae the spiritual child typically assumes, including the dramatist, naturalist, artist and spiritual awakener of transformative learning using technology, specifically tablets, as a component for understanding children's spirituality. This exploratory study summarises children's perceptions and early childhood student educators' reflections of photos taken by young children using tablets while exploring nature and the outdoors. Digital photos using tablets and taken by young children encouraged descriptive conversations and connections about their world and also provide a framework for future early childhood educators to consider regarding the spiritual domain through children's eyes.

The role of spirituality

The definition of spirituality, which has been a continuous topic in education (Wane 2011), is dependent upon one's worldview (Cole 2011). Spirituality has multiple definitions, some of them centring on a personal relationship with the divine, others remaining secular, for example, organising the story of one's life (Allen 2008; Bennett 2003; Housekamp, Fisher, and Stuber 2004). Spirituality is often connected with awe, wonder, love and mystery (Earl 2001). It can also involve knowing much more than physical or worldly existence and feeling engulfed by an infinite source of creativity, interconnectedness and diverse expressions of life (Richmond-Bravo 2011). Ultimately, spirituality is about personal empowerment, personal and collective transformation, and relationships (Ritskes 2011) and encompasses all that is human: spirituality nurtures, sustains and moulds the presence of human lives (King 2013). As a critical part of human nature (Cupit 2004) and an internal force that guides people's lives, spirituality incorporates values, traditions, beliefs and unique experiences (L. Hart 2011). Thus, the spiritual journey allows people to achieve wholeness and the power to develop their inner force through life's journey (Wane 2011).

The spiritual domain of young children

According to a general consensus, spirituality has profound importance for children (Zhang and Wu 2012). A young child's spirituality may be one of the most contemplative customs helping to understand that humans know beyond what is seen (Miller 2015). The touch points for the spiritual being are found in childhood (Hart 2003). In fact, in many countries, awareness of spiritual development is included in the school curriculum. For example, countries that promote opportunities for spiritual development in the classroom include Australia and New Zealand (Zhang and Wu 2012). In addition, in the United Kingdom, the 2011 Education Act mandated that schools promote children's spiritual development (HM Government 2011).

Young children have unique spiritual lives (Hart 2003), in which they can be conscious or unconscious participants (Mueller 2010). In most cases, they express their spirituality primarily through behaviours, and teachers can understand much of what young children are experiencing through the observation of the children's behaviours (Myers, 1997). For example, young children use a variety of symbols in dramatic play and creative movements during dance and creative movement to express joy, happiness and awe. During pretend play, children make value judgements with peers and question meaning in daily experiences. Research has shown that spirituality may play an important part in a child's daily life, serving as a protective shield in the form of resilience, which can intensify during times of crisis, emotional distress or criticism of one's culture (Barnes et al. 2000). Qualities identifying the spiritual domain include compassion, acceptance, mindfulness, a sense of oneness with all and an innate association to nature (Miller 2015). Because of this, it is critical to explore the spiritual potential of childhood for their healthy, holistic well-being (King 2013).

Children's spirituality is intrinsic to their process of growth and change. Children seem to have a natural spirituality revealed in their sense of wonder, their fantasies and imagination, their play and their curiosity (Waite and Halstead 2001). In supporting the development and education of the whole child, one should include thoughtful consideration of children's spiritual development (Baumgartner and Buchanan 2010). While early childhood may be considered a spiritually significant experience, the personae and perspective of the spiritual child has customarily not attracted much attention (King 2013).

Technology and spirituality

The way we view our world today has changed due to the rapid advances in technology (Cotto 2015). Technology is growing exponentially every day (Sharapan 2015). With increased availability to tablets in homes and early childhood settings, young children are spending a substantial amount of time using tablets for entertainment and educational purposes (Neumann and Neumann 2017). Technology can be compared to the ground upon which we breathe and build the foundations of our lives and our spirituality (Spyker 2007). As a result, technology has transformed our world by getting us to our final destination more quickly, but many times, succeeding only in making life more hectic and a yearning to slow down (Spyker 2007). For parents and teachers who live in a world filled with tablets, smart phones, handheld digital games and other mobile devices, making effective and appropriate choices regarding the use of technology tools can be difficult (Donohue 2015). However, when used appropriately, technology can be an effective tool to support learning and foster digital citizenship (Donohue 2015).

American television personality, writer, producer and Presbyterian Minister Fred Rogers approached technology as an invitation to work together and collaborate with one another (Sharapan 2015). His educational preschool television show, *Mister Rogers' Neighborhood* (1968–2001), created a 'neighborhood' theme that taught children to understand the value of relationships with families, friends and peers in the child's community. Mr Rogers used technology as a means to support people connect and interact with each other (Sharapan 2015). When reflecting and considering the neighbourhood, Fred Rogers modelled to young audiences the idea of technology and spirituality blending together could have the ability to affect one another regarding the importance of relationships, developing empathy and self-efficacy. Relationships are spiritual events just as ongoing interactions for spiritual connection and attainment (Miller 2015). As new technology becomes accessible to families, children can stay connected with family members at all times strengthening community through frequent communications, both online and offline (Cotto 2015).

Tablets as supporting and empowering spiritual tool

When used in ways that support educational goals for young children, technology tools such as tablets can offer unique functions, abundant applications and more flexibility for personal expression and learning (Blagojevic and Thomes 2008). Tablets are highly versatile and user-friendly for young children (Arnott, Grogan, and Duncan 2016). Tablets differ from traditional desktop computers in that they are mobile, handheld devices with a user-friendly interface touch screen (Neumann and Neumann 2014). As a result, children are able to use tablets relatively with ease and comfort for exploring new skills, taking photos and collaboration between peers during play (McManis and Gunnewig 2012).

Recent research also suggests that tablets support children's learning having a positive impact on children's engagement, motivation, independence and self-regulation (Clark and Luckin 2013). For example, photos taken with tablets can offer children opportunities to interact with peers and also increase children's interests and confidence in expressing their views (Blagojevic and Thomes 2008). A teacher could promote conversations among peers by inviting pairs or small groups of children to view pictures taken and discuss what they liked best or remembered about an activity. As this happens, the tablet becomes a window onto a new way of seeing (Paintner 2013). Tablets also have the ability to enhance as well as transform many learning activities for young children (Bailey and Blagojevic 2015). For example, tablets can provide opportunities for children to observe their world from a new perspective, focus on and identify specific elements within the environment, and document their learning activities both in the classroom and at home. Photos taken with tablets can embrace a child's heart and be captured as a memory with meaning and comfort for a lifetime. Finally, tablets may offer a promising spring board for children's involvement in research processes and can be a method for young children to express and voice their creativity (Arnott, Grogan, and Duncan 2016).

Research question and methodology

To explore and contribute knowledge to this topic, an exploratory study was conducted at a child development lab school in the Midwest with early childhood educators. As such, qualitative inquiry (Creswell 2012) provided the enriching data required. During the exploratory study, early childhood educators' and young children aged 3–5 observed the outdoor world using tablets. Research suggests mobile technology, such as tablets, as a useful tool in early childhood education, and with proper introduction and scaffolding by teachers, can make a positive impact on children's learning (Neumann and Neumann 2014). Furthermore, limited research has investigated the use of tablets for very young children in preschool educational settings (Crescenzi, Jewitt, and Price 2014). In this study, the author investigates how technology, especially the use of tablets, and allowing children to be active participants in the research process, can be an engaging process for both the child and the early childhood student educator. The study also introduces how photography can be one approach to encourage and nurture a child's spiritual development by empowering children to be self-sufficient research participants while using tablets as part of the data collection process. Throughout their time together, children were invited to take photos that were meaningful and purposeful to them. These photos touched the hearts, minds and spirits of young children. Part of our spiritual journey is learning how to see, not only with our physical eyes, but also with our spiritual eyes (Paintner 2013).

Awakening spiritual awareness using tablets outdoors

Fourteen early childhood student educators' and 20 young children aged 3–5 at a child development lab school in the Midwest of the United States took a field trip to observe the outdoor world on campus by taking photographs with tablets on a fall morning. The outdoor environment was selected because nature is the most fundamental and original spiritual community for children (Miller 2015). Nature-based activities provide direct, multimodal and multi-sensory interactions with natural elements and living things (Singer et al. 2009). Children are absorbed by nature; the sense of a caring relationship with all living things is spiritual (Miller 2015). Exploring and playing outdoors can provide young children a level of comfort and freedom not found in the classroom, which in turn may build confidence and a sense of well-being (Flynn and Kieff 2002). During their time together, children were invited to take photographs of their favourite interests on their own accompanied by an early childhood student educator. The children's desire to use the tablets to take photos promoted interest in the project. As children took photos, the early childhood student educators observed children's overt behaviours and asked open-ended questions to investigate their sensory awareness regarding the photographs being taken.

Teachers' supporting role with using technology

When considering the use of technology for young children, teachers have a very supporting role and are responsible for the appropriate and beneficial use of technology. Preparing to teach with technology, especially in early childhood settings, requires collaboration and support through the learning process (Gilbert and Cristol 2004). Therefore, it is critical that teachers use technology carefully, appropriately and intentionally (Jung and Conderman 2015). During the on-site field trip, guidelines were followed to increase spiritual learning opportunities using tablets. First, the early childhood student educators provided a safe and open area and space on campus for the children to investigate and explore. Young children from the lab school were introduced to tablets and given ample time to sightsee, revisit, pay close attention to and reflect on the photos they were taking with the early childhood student. During the exploratory study, early childhood educator students were intentionally present using open-ended questions and focusing on the child's lead and interests. The student educators used active listening skills including close eye contact, I/we messages, paraphrasing and verbal prompting and assisting in close proximity to engage and participate with children throughout the activity. Student educators listened to children's perspectives and followed the child's lead based on the interests and needs of each child. As they shared ideas and asked questions, children's natural curiosity and wonder emerged making them feel more comfortable using the tablets and making connections outdoors. Because of the attraction and familiarity of using tablets at the lab school for instruction and alongside their play with peers during discovery time, tablets were transformed from a teacher-centred to a user-friendly, child-centred learning tool that was accessible and flexible for all children. During the exploratory study, outdoor experiences were child-led, whereby engagement with the tablets were dictated by the young children. Providing the children with control over the tablets created opportunities for autonomy and offered a guide for self-expression, while having the child at the centre of the process. For example, the flexibility of the tablet for taking pictures allowed children to place the tablet on a leaf or blade of grass, next to a flower, on top of a tree branch or prop it up to take a picture from their level of sight. The photos taken gave children first-hand data about their photo experiences. At the conclusion of the exploratory study, early childhood educator students documented conversations and stories with children and reflected on sharing an intimate glimpse into the variety of themes representing the personae of the spiritual child.

The personae of the spiritual child as a dramatist filled with wonder

A young child's world is filled with the magic of exploration, discovery, make-believe and play (Klein, Wirth, and Linas 2003). Childhood is a time of wonder and awe (Hart 2003). One of the hallmarks of early childhood, wonder is a principal source of humanity's spiritual impulse (Fuller 2006). Wonder refers to the way in which young children sense the world and involves an array of feelings, such as connection, insight and awe as well as a sense of joy (Hyde 2008). All spiritual life begins with and is nourished by a sense of wonder (Louv 2012). Never hesitating to wonder out loud, the spiritual child is a self-motivated, active learner who reflects on discoveries.

For the spiritual child, wonder is characterised by a strong sense of the fullness of the present. This was evident during the photo activity. Under supervision, young children wondered on their own and with the early childhood student educator about the buildings on campus, the sound of fallen apples from trees, plants growing under trees, dandelions, acorns and seeds they found on the grass, shadows of themselves and light between trees, and campus artefact such as various art sculptures near parts of the entry ways on campus. Two children were also enthralled by the different rocks they found comparing the textures and sizes. One early childhood educator commented,

My child loved pointing at certain things in nature and posing next to them. I loved how in some instances, she couldn't find a specific vocabulary word for the object she was trying to describe, so she would relate it to a story, song, television show, or simply called it what it looked like. What I admired most was the bravery of the children. They were unafraid to run, to climb, to walk upon moving swings, to take risks. I miss that part of childhood.

Childhood moments of wonder are not merely passing reveries; they can be both small and tremendous. Moments of wonder shape the way a child understands the world. For example, one student stated, 'I would never have expected a child this young would focus so much on the ground, instead of the larger, more colorful objects to be found around us'. Another student explained, 'Both of my children were enthralled with rocks and dirt, so much so that they were climbing all over the rocks and searching for worms in the dirt'. Mystical or powerful transcendent moments of awareness are common to the spiritual child because of innate closeness to spiritual awareness in the universe (Miller 2015). These connections are true and valuable to them.

Wonder readily enables the spiritual child to become capable of true empathy or kindness (Fuller 2006). These moments are often the core of a child's spiritual identity (Hart 2003). For example, one early childhood student stated,

> Lilly was first excited to jump in muddy puddle before seeing her friends on swings. She loved swinging with her friends and took a picture of her friends while swinging. She said that was her favorite picture because her friends were smiling and having fun.

The spiritual child often sees reciprocity in a world that is built with inherent sense (Miller 2015). Those message and visions, then, become the living words of the spiritual child.

Children guide others by reminding them that they live in a vast sea of wonder and mystery (Hart 2003). Wonder brings joy; for spiritual children, wonder has the capacity to allow them to escape egocentric orientation and enable them to see more fully the needs and interests of others (Fuller 2006). For example, one student documented, 'Each time Christopher would take a picture he would pull it up so he could see the bigger view and then he would say, "OOO it is a pretty picture." Wonder is nourished by opportunities to observe the intricacies of nature (Wolf 1996). One child loved the picture of the grass she took because, 'the grass is pretty'. As spiritual children attend to their experiences and the wonder inherent in them, they have the opportunity to engage in mindful awareness of the world. In other words, being present in the moment. Through this experience of wonder, children aspire to become unique individuals and true citizens of the universe (De Pascuale 2003, September). The spiritual child is aware of the universe and the cycles of nature and knows that all nature moves in cycles.

The personae of the spiritual child as a naturist and visionary seeing beauty in life

The spiritual child has a strong affinity for nature (Crain 2003). At one point during the activity, one child was flying around like a butterfly and said, 'I'm an orange and black butterfly'. Young children have an inborn love of nature (Kahn 1999); for example, infants and toddlers often express joy when visiting the zoo or catching sight of a puppy when playing with friends. Smiles appears and laughter erupts when playing with a dog, holding a kitten, feeding birds with a family member or watching a deer from a classroom window with peers. Young children are energised by nature when making sand castles, walking the seashore and examining seashells, making mud pies, watching clouds and playing with water. For example, during investigations while taking photos, two girls spotted a pile of leaves and started working together and pushing them together so they could jump into the pile. The early childhood student commented, 'You could definitely see the happiness in their eyes about their surroundings when they snapped their own photographs outdoors with the tablet'. Another child just wanted to skip and stated to the early childhood student, 'Follow me!' The student commented,

> I found it really fun to take the pictures of Sarah. She loved to climb the big rocks and be on the swings. I got some interesting pictures of what she loved to look at and the expression on her face. To me, I truly did capture what Sarah was seeing in the world by the look on her face.

In nature, a child finds freedom, fantasy and privacy; a place distant from the adult world, a separate place to dream, play, find solitude and feel joyful (Louv 2005). One child loved the sun shining onto the lawn and through the buildings on campus. The early childhood student commented, 'Seeing the joy in Tamara's eyes made me want to capture and relive those moments, and by taking photos on the tablet, I am able to do just that'. During the photo activity, one boy took several pictures of wildflowers. While taking the pictures, he discovered interest in the multiple colours and different-shaped leaves and number of petals. After the activity, he took time to find a book about flowers so he could put names with the photographs. Two friends also enjoyed running in and out of the trees because the trees had long leaves and would hide them from their friends. The children commented to the early childhood student, 'SHH, be quiet! They can't know we are here'. The early childhood student commented, 'Using their imagination is something truly amazing! You can make the area into anything you can think of if you put your mind to it!'

Nature motivates children's powers of observation and instils feelings of peace and oneness with the world (Crain 2003). In addition, nature can bring feelings of calmness and freshness of perception to children by instilling a sense of peace. One early childhood student commented, 'Before they started taking pictures, Nancy stood in awe and looked at the surroundings'. Nature stimuli are often subtle, mild and calming to children (Hanscom 2016). When young children are given opportunities to explore nature near forests, parks, ponds and wooded fields, they are in the midst of a very nurturing presence in which they can truly make original discoveries involving all the senses. Such moments as these can produce the creation of new neurons, the brain cells that process and transmit information. In many cases, it is reasonable to imagine that time spent in nature restores and stimulates the spiritual child with new neurons – 'nature neurons' that produce energy and creativity (Louv 2012). During these particular moments, the spiritual child can feel a deep connection to nature. The child, therefore, can use the power of nature to stimulate learning and creativity. One student remarked,

> It made me feel like a child again. I will always treasure the pictures Alice and Marilyn took on my tablet. They started pointing to everything and wanted to take pictures of everything. I loved the fact that they were so carefree.

Family members and teachers should consider these opportunities to stimulate the spiritual child's curiosity as a naturalist and visionary for kindred spirits. Learning about the natural world should be seen as one of the most important and mindful processes in children's lives.

The personae of the spiritual child as creative artist

The creative energy of the spiritual child is an outward expression of his or her spirit (Wolf 1996). By observing and listening to the spiritual child, the teacher can learn the child's special interests, what lights up her eyes or captures his attention. One's interests and passions often reveal character and calling (Hart 2003). Drawing, dancing, painting, singing, pretending, acting and constructing are all expressions of a spiritual child's zest for life. The architecture of a spiritual life includes the structure of delight (Hart 2003). The spiritual child often displays delight and creativity so effortlessly. For example, one child was so excited taking pictures, she told the student, 'I love my pictures because they are beautiful and I can look at them over and over again'. Her favourite pictures were pictures of clouds and pictures of herself with a friend playing near the art sculptures. The child recreated several pictures later in the classroom using markers and crayons. In a moment of time, the child is engaged using all senses, working independently with intense focus and often making meaningful connections with peers. Intangible and characterised by exploration of possibilities and producing meaning, creativity and spiritual knowledge are closely linked (Villaverde 1999).

When the spiritual child takes time to reflect and carefully look at works of art, she or he opens up opportunities to tell stories, share meaningful experiences, imagine and explore. Learning begins with the child's 'human sense', which is the understanding of the world constructed through experience (Donaldson 1978). By looking at artwork from a variety of perspectives, the spiritual child has the potential to become open-minded and accepting of diverse ways of thinking (Greene 1995). As an artist, the spiritual child looks at artwork closely. This child is curious and will often take risks, wondering about his or her work and asking, 'What if?', What if I added another colour? What if I made a purple donkey with a polka dot tail? What if I added glitter to the rainbow? The spiritual child delights in playful words, dreams big and imagines the 'what if' by taking time for learning instead of simply doing. For example, after the field trip, several children made fireworks using cut toilet paper rolls and paint. Other children painted self-portraits and pictures using open-ended materials they found, thanks to Mother Nature, such as small pinecones, rocks, acorns, leaves, large chucks of dirt and small branches.

The personae of the spiritual child as an awakener of transformative learning

According to Dewey (1916), a child's individual instinct and powers of awareness and interest furnish the materials and lay the foundation for all education. Children become aware very early that through the art of research, they can discover the joy of living. The spiritual child learns with real-life sensory experiences and open-ended materials. Much of children's early learning comes through self-discovery, an outcome of play (Klein, Wirth, and Linas 2003). This was demonstrated during the field trip as children pretended the bookstore was a castle and the bench swings were a pirate ship. One child told his friends that he could not leave the ship because the sharks would come to take the hidden treasures. Two other children were pretending to be spies by running from tree to tree between shadows of the leaves to capture their friends. This was documented by one early childhood student, 'Towards the end of our journey, the girls were singing with each other, skipping around the lawn, and acting like mummies inside of the sculptures'. This type of educational experience encourages independent thinking, a zest for learning and joy in living. The spiritual child, who has the ability to construct a global world of knowledge and then later convey what they know to others in a confident and joyful manner, is a competent learner. A child's sense of self is the origin of his or her spirituality (Cole 2011).

Transformative education empowers children to find their inner voices and power (Gardner and Kelly 2008); its primary goal is to influence social change through self-empowerment (Gardner and Kelly 2008). Providing opportunities to reflect on their ideas and beliefs, transformative education encourages children to become critical thinkers (Mezirow 2003) and nurtures the whole child (Hart 2011). In addition, transformative education empowers spiritual children to desire to understand the why instead of simply reproducing knowledge, allows a silenced voice to be heard, and motivates spiritual children to raise ideas and questions relevant and important in their lives. When a child is able to connect with the heart and the spirit, change is possible in the lives of children (Hart 2011).

The spiritual child embraces learning with the heart, body and soul. One early childhood student commented,

> If students were interested in taking pictures, teachers could use these images to discover the children's passions and see what they are interested in. By talking with the children about their pictures, teachers can dig into the souls of children and discover how to get through to them

The soul can be nurtured through cooperative learning, creative thinking and personal reflection (Hart 2011). Because learning includes personal experiences and social awareness, learning for the spiritual child becomes more meaningful and engaging. Holistic learning for the spiritual child is enlivened when she or he is given space to be authentic and to share passions and interests. This authentic self can be discovered through play, the arts, reflection and dialogue (Kessler 2000). Giving young children time to engage in free play is like presenting them with a special gift. This gift keeps on giving, preparing children for their next journey for adulthood by nurturing essential life skills (Hanscom 2016). The awakened spirit of the spiritual child brings learning to life and allows the child to form engaging connections with peers by sharing life stories with opportunities to question and discover. The spiritual child has the energy and enthusiasm to embrace the world with awareness, skills, questions and voice. This type of learning occurs continuously, joyously and both arduously and effortlessly (Fried 2001).

Conclusion

Waite and Halstead (2001) concluded that,

> young children are naturally spiritual, citing their sense of wonder and fascination with things, their extraordinary capacity to play, to enter into fantasy, to exercise their imagination, their intense awareness of immediate experiences and emotions, and their innocent raising of profound questions about the meaning of life (p. 185).

Children have powerful thoughts about the world and how it works (2008). A child's spiritual development builds respect, compassion, humility and gentleness, and strengthens the entire self and the human spirit of the learner (Dei 2002). Opportunities to channel their spiritual energy constructively and to explore their dreams and passions with peers and nurturing elders will support balance, integrity, meaning and connection in their lives (Kessler 2000). Spiritual education must be seen as valuable in its own right and not merely as a way of improving the morals of the nation's young people

(Kibble 1996). For this exploratory study, young children explored and captured with early childhood student educators how technology, specifically tablets, supports meaningful learning. Throughout the activity, children maintained a high level of interest in using the tablets for taking pictures and documenting pictures of personal importance. Children were engaged and at times, friendships between children increased interactions and participation. Children's spiritual discoveries during this project became a springboard for later learning and teachable spiritual moments.

Children's fascination with using technology during this project gave the student educators opportunities to intentionally listen to children's ideas, feelings and thought processes. Table 1. summarises reflections and thoughtful comments from early childhood student educators regarding this field trip. The journey into taking photos outdoors and embracing nature as a reflective, teaching tool is a journey towards seeing the world as it really is (Paintner 2013). Young children have a natural richness with the world around them; the child is born with this assumed relationship with all of nature, from goslings to galaxies (Miller, 2015). There is a theoretical perspective that defines spiritual development as an integral component of every child's life (Myers, 1997). Consequently, young children should be guided to explore their

Table 1. Reflections from early childhood students taking pictures of the heart using tablets.

- 'This activity has been a valuable reminder to me as to what teachers can do if they only think outside the box a little'.
- 'There is so much wonder a photo can leave with you, and there are so many unanswered questions you can have when you look at a photo'.
- 'It is great to see how one picture is not the same, all pictures are different and there is a purpose behind them'.
- 'I loved this activity because it gave me a chance to look through the child's eyes and see the different variety of objects that caught their attention'.
- 'I think that this type of activity is beneficial for children because it allows them to pay attention to details and things they would not normally notice in a typical classroom setting'.
- 'My child wanted to touch materials and reach out to nature that was found and she liked to use the tablet to take pictures. As the teacher, I found a common ground for both of them'.
- 'Taking time out of the day and giving children the opportunity to take pictures of their surroundings and things that they find interesting is very empowering and inspiring for children. Taking pictures on the tablet is another way to express creative arts with children. It is also a type of stress reliever'.
- 'Maria and Amy really showed me the importance and the innocence in life. Now that I am reflecting on my experience, I am really thinking about what's important in life. The photography made both of the girls so happy, and they were a true joy to be around. When children see wonder, the world reveals its wonder to us'.
- 'Reflecting on the photos is important because it allows for you to express what you have observed and learned from the experience. Taking time to reflect allows you to grow through your experiences. Using the tablets to take photos is a great way for children to express themselves to creatively share their perspective in life'.
- 'Photography is a great way to revisit moments, but it also a great way to capture in feelings in the moment, experiences, and events. By taking photos of nature, sunshine, and people, you are able to relive and revisit things you love'.
- 'I believe photography is a wonderful way for children to learn and it allows them to express themselves through a different type of media. Photography gives children a voice and allows them to use their creativity and decision-making skills. As teachers, we need to remember that we should not tell the child what to photograph, we should allow them make the decisions and keep their photography as open-ended as possible. Let them explore and be the artist!'
- 'Based on this experience, I would most definitely incorporate photography and nature into my future classroom'.

holistic spiritual identity, discover its meaning and connect to others through their understanding of the world (Cole 2011). The holistic dimensions of the spiritual child with love and respect speak not only to the corporal child but also to the child within, the mystic child, the magical child (Stairs 2000). In using technology, the tablet becomes a creative tool to develop our ability to see more deeply, more clearly and to see the child's vision of the world and through the eyes of the soul and emotion (Paintner 2013).

Disclosure statement

No potential conflict of interest was reported by the author.

References

Allen, H. C. 2008. "Exploring Children's Spirituality from a Christian Perspective." In *Nurturing Children's Spirituality*, Ed. H. C. Allen, 1–20. Eugene, OR: Cascade.
Arnott, L., D. Grogan, and P. Duncan. 2016. "Lessons from Using iPads to Understand Young Children's Creativity." *Contemporary Issues in Early Childhood* 17 (2): 157–173. doi:10.1177/1463949116633347.
Bailey, M., and B. Blagojevic. 2015. "Innovate, Educate, and Empower: New Opportunities with New Technologies." In *Technology and Digital Media in the Early Years: Tools for Teaching and Learning*, Ed. C. Donohue, 162–171. New York, NY: Routledge.
Barnes, L. L., G. A. Plotnikof, K. Fox, and S. Pendleton. 2000. "Subject Reviews: Spirituality and Foster Care, Spirituality, Religion, and Pediatrics: Intersecting Worlds of Healing." *Pediatrics* 104 (6): 899–908.
Baumgartner, J. J., and T. Buchanan. 2010. "Supporting Each Child's Spirit." *Young Children* 65 (2): 90–95.
Bennett, J. B. 2003. *Academic Life: Hospitality, Ethics, and Spirituality*. Boston, MA: Anker.
Blagojevic, B., and K. Thomes. 2008. "Young Photographers." *Young Children* 63 (5): 66–72.
Clark, W., and R. Luckin (2013). What the Research says – iPads in the Classroom. July 25, 2017.http://digitalteachingandlearning.files.workpress.com/2013/03/iPads-in-the-classroom-reportlkl.pdf
Cole, J. 2011. "Situating Children in the Discourse of Spirituality." In *Spirituality, Education, and Society*, Eds. N. N. Wane, E. L. Manyimo, and E. J. Ritskes, 1–14. Boston, MA: Sense Publishers.
Cotto, L. M. 2015. "Technology as a Tool to Strengthen the Community." In *Technology and Digital Media in the Early Years: Tools for Teaching and Learning*, Ed. C. Donohue, 162–171. New York, NY: Routledge.
Crain, W. 2003. *Reclaiming Childhood: Letting Children Be Children in Our Achievement-Oriented Society*. New York, NY: Henry Holt.
Crescenzi, L., C. Jewitt, and S. Price. 2014. "The Role of Touch in Preschool Children's Learning Using iPad versus Paper Interaction." *Australian Journal of Language and Literacy* 37 (2): 86—95.

Creswell, J. W. 2012. *Qualitative Inquiry and Research Design: Choosing among Five Approaches*. Thousand Oaks, CA: SAGE.

Cupit, C. G. 2004. "Criteria for a Comprehensive Model for Spiritual Development in Secular Educative Care." *International Journal of Children's Spirituality* 9 (3): 293–305. doi:10.1080/1364436042000292202.

De Pascuale, J. (2003, September). A Wonder Full Life. *Notre Dame Magazine*, 49.

Dei, G. 2002. "Learning Culture, Spirituality, and Local Knowledge: Implications for African Schooling." *International Review of Education* 48 (5): 335–360. doi:10.1023/A:1021283730231.

Dewey, J. 1916. *Democracy and Education*. New York, NY: Free Press.

Donaldson, M. 1978. *Children's Minds*. New York, NY: Norton.

Donohue, C. 2015. "Technology and Digital Media as Tools for Teaching and Learning in the Digital Age." In *Technology and Digital Media in the Early Years: Tools for Teaching and Learning*, Ed. C. Donohue, 21–35. New York, NY: Routledge.

Earl, M. 2001. "Shadow and Spirituality." *International Journal of Children's Spirituality* 6 (3): 277–288. doi:10.1080/13644360120100450.

Flynn, L. L., and J. Kieff. 2002. "Including Everyone in Outdoor Play." *Young Children* 57 (3): 20–30.

Fried, R. L. 2001. *The Passionate Learner: How Teachers and Parents Can Help Children Reclaim the Joy of Discovery*. Boston, MA: Bacon Press.

Fuller, R. C. 2006. *Wonder from Emotion to Spirituality*. Chapel Hill, NC: University of North Carolina Press.

Gardner, M., and U. Kelly. 2008. *Narrating Transformative Learning in Education*. Toronto Canada: Palgrave MacMillan.

Gilbert, B., and D. Cristol. 2004. "Teaching Curriculum with Technology: Enhancing Children's Technological Competence during Early Childhood." *Early Childhood Education Journal* 31 (3): 207–216.

Greene, M. 1995. *Releasing the Imagination*. San Francisco, CA: Jossey-Bass.

Hanscom, A. J. 2016. *Balanced and Barefoot*. Oakland, CA: New Harbinger Publications.

Hart, L. 2011. "Nourishing the Authentic Self: Teaching with Heart and Soul." In *Spirituality, Education, and Society*, Eds. N. N. Wane, E. L. Manyimo, and E. J. Ritskes, 37–48. Boston, MA: Sense Publishers.

Hart, T. 2003. *The Secret Spiritual World of Children*. Novato, CA: New World Library.

HM Government. 2011. *Education Act 2011*. London, UK: Author.

Housekamp, B., L. Fisher, and M. Stuber. 2004. "Spirituality in Children and Adolescents: Research Finding and Implications for Clinicians and Researchers." *Child and Adolescent Psychiatric Conics of North America* 13: 221–230. doi:10.1016/S1056-4993(03)00072-5.

Hyde, B. 2008. *Children's Spirituality: Searching for Meaning and Connectedness*. Philadelphia, PA: Jessica Kingsley.

Jung, G., and G. Conderman. 2015. "Using Digital Technology to Support Mathematics Instruction." *Young Children* 70 (3): 64—69.

Kahn, P. H. 1999. *The Human Relationship to Nature*. Cambridge, MA: MIT Press.

Kessler, R. 2000. *The Soul of Education: Helping Students Find Connection, Compassion and Character at School*. Alexandria, VA: Association for Supervision and Curriculum Development.

Kibble, D. G. 1996. "Spiritual Development, Spiritual Experience and Spiritual Education." In *Education, Spirituality, and the Whole Child*, Ed. R. Best, 64–74. New York, NY: Cassell.

King, U. 2013. "The Spiritual Potential of Childhood: Awakening to the Fullest of Life." *International Journal of Children's Spirituality* 18 (1): 4–17. doi:10.1080/1364436X.2013.776266.

Klein, T. P., D. Wirth, and K. Linas. 2003. "Play: Children's Context for Development." *Young Children* 58 (3): 38–45.

Louv, R. 2005. *Last Child in the Woods: Saving Our Children from Nature-Deficit Disorder*. Chapel Hill, NC: Algonquin Books of Chapel Hill.

Louv, R. 2012. *The Nature Principle: Reconnecting with Life in a Virtual Age*. Chapel Hill, NC: Algonquin Books of Chapel Hill.

McManis, L. D., and S. B. Gunnewig. 2012. "Finding the Education in Educational Technology with Early Learners." *Young Children* 67 (3): 14–24.

Mezirow, J. 2003. "Transformative Learning as Discourse." *Journal of Transformative Education* 1 (1): 58–63. doi:10.1177/1541344603252172.

Miller, L. (2015). The spiritual child: The new science on parenting for health and life long thriving" is listed in the reference section.

Miller, L. 2015. *The Spiritual Child: The New Science on Parenting for Health and Lifelong Thriving*. New York, NY: St. Martin's Press.

Mueller, C. R. 2010. "Spirituality in Children: Understanding and Developing Interventions." *Pediatric Nursing* 36 (4): 197–208.

Myers, B. K. 1997. *Young Children and Spirituality*. New York, NY: Routledge.

Neumann, M. M., and D. L. Neumann. 2014. "Touch Screen Tablets and Emergent Literacy." *Early Childhood Education Journal* 42 (4): 231–239. doi:10.1007/s10643-013-0608-3.

Neumann, M. M., and D. L. Neumann. 2017. "The Use of Touch-Screen Tablets at Home and Pre-School to Foster Emergent Literacy." *Journal of Early Childhood Literacy* 17 (2): 203–220. doi:10.1177/1468798415619773.

Paintner, C. V. 2013. *Eyes of the Heart*. Notre Dame, IN: Sorin Books.

Richmond-Bravo, J. 2011. "Wisdom Sharing and Altered Consciousness: A Transformative Learning Project." In *Spirituality, Education, and Society*, Eds. N. N. Wane, E. L. Manyimo, and E. J. Ritskes, 219–234. Boston, MA: Sense Publishers.

Ritskes, E. J. 2011. "Connected: Indigenous Spirituality as Resistance in the Classroom." In *Spirituality, Education, and Society*, Eds. N. N. Wane, E. L. Manyimo, and E. J. Ritskes, 15–36. Boston, MA: Sense Publishers.

Sharapan, H. 2015. "Technology as a Tool for Social–Emotional Development: What We Can Learn from Fred Rogers' Approach." In *Technology and Digital Media in the Early Years: Tools for Teaching and Learning*, Ed. C. Donohue, 12–20. New York, NY: Routledge.

Singer, D. G., J. L. Singer, R. D'Agostino, and R. DeLong. 2009. "Children's past Times and Play in Sixteen Nations: Is Free-Play Declining?" *American Journal of Play* 1 (3): 283–312.

Spyker, S. K. 2007. *Technology & Spirituality: How the Information Revolution Affects Our Spiritual Lives*. Woodstock, Vermont: Skylight Path.

Stairs, J. 2000. *Listening for the Soul*. Minneapolis, MN: Fortress Press.

Villaverde, L. 1999. "Creativity, Art, and Aesthetics Unraveled through Post-Formalism: An Exploration of Perception, Experience, and Pedagogy." In *The Post-Formal Reader: Cognition and Education*, edited by S. R. Steinberg, J. L. Kincheloe, and P. H. Hinchey. NewYork, NY: Falmer Press.

Waite, S., and M. Halstead. 2001. "Nurturing the Spiritual in Children's Sexual Development." *International Journal of Children's Spirituality* 6 (2): 185–206. doi:10.1080/13644360124584.

Wane, N. N. 2011. "Spirituality: A Philosophy and A Research Tool." In *Spirituality, Education, and Society*, Eds. N. N. Wane, E. L. Manyimo, and E. J. Ritskes, 67–82. Boston, MA: Sense Publishers.

Wolf, A. D. 1996. *Nurturing the Spirit in Non-Sectarian Classrooms*. Santa Rosa, CA: Parent Child Press.

Zhang, K. C., and D. I. Wu. 2012. "Nurturing the Spiritual Well-Being of Children with Special Needs." *Support for Learning: British Journal of Learning Support* 27 (3): 119–122. doi:10.1111/j.1467-9604.2012.01528.x.

Cyber spirituality: Facebook, Twitter, and the adolescent quest for connection

Karen-Marie Yust, Brendan Hyde and Cathy Ota

Two of us have spent time on Facebook recently with adolescent children. Brendan discovered that he would have to create an account with Facebook to view photographs of a local musical in which he had been involved, since the photographs had been uploaded onto the amateur group's Facebook page on the Internet. Being unfamiliar with such technology, he enlisted the help of his 16-year-old son to create the account. No sooner had he done this, than he was inundated with emails from 'the Facebook Team' (who are they, he wondered) informing him that various people (some of whom he knew, others total strangers) had seen his 'wall' and wanted him to add them as friends. Curiosity got the better of him, and so, with the help of his son, he added them as friends – again to the inundation of emails from the Facebook Team confirming that these people were now his 'new' friends on Facebook and with the offer to add other people whom he may or may not know as further new friends. To the amusement of his son, he threw up his hands with a look of total bewilderment. 'It's ok dad', his son said reassuringly, 'I have over 200 friends on Facebook'.

Karen-Marie, who has had a Facebook account for over three years, logged in on her birthday to a chorus of cyber well wishes, many from the friends of her adolescent children. Classmates of her 19-year-old daughter and 16-year-old son have also shared snippets of information about their activities, tagged her in photographs taken during move-in day at university and the secondary school's Fall Festival, and 'chatted' with her through Facebook's instance messaging function. Colleagues' children – some of whom she has known since early childhood – have 'friended' her and comment on her wall postings or include her in the various games and surveys friends can exchange with one another. She could easily spend several hours a week on Facebook interacting with these young people, were she not so busy with her face-to-face life in Richmond.

The phenomenon of social networking intrigues us. We wonder how this technological advancement, which has the ability to connect young people to one another and with adults without regard for geographic or national boundaries, is shaping the spiritual lives of young people. The amount of time many spend on Facebook and Twitter (another derivative of this type of communication) suggests that social networking may be experienced as a type of cyber spirituality that enables them to apperceive some sense of connectedness with other like-minded seekers. The Center for Spiritual Development in Childhood and Adolescence has identified 'connecting and belonging' as a key theme for spiritual development. Roehlkepartain and his colleagues (2008) quote a 14-year-old American girl, who explains, 'Being spiritual is when you have a connection, and you can feel how other people are feeling, and you understand their thoughts and their emotions.' As 'digital natives' (persons who have always had computers at hand), adolescents view laptops and 'smart' phones (mobiles with

Internet capability) as just another tool they may use for spiritual purposes. When they share their 'status' (current activity or emotion) on Facebook and follow the 'threads' (postings and responses) of others, they tune into the thoughts and feelings of a diverse group of people who may function as a 'community of the heart' that brings 'memory, feeling, imagination, and thinking' together to shape the human spirit (Ford 1997).

Furthermore, Facebook activity between adolescents and parents or other adults can provide opportunities for influence and guidance by spiritual role models and mentors. Roehlkepartain et al.'s study (2008) found that between 61 and 76% of the more than 6500 young people they surveyed in eight countries relied on parents or other adult figures to help them with spiritual development. Smith's (2009) research tracking religiosity from adolescence to young adulthood in American teens points to relationships with 'many supportive religious adults' as a consistently important factor in continued faith and religious practice among emerging adults. He argues that the maintenance of strong relationships with adults as adolescents mature and leave home may be a major causal mechanism underlying this finding. While we can find no studies of the efficacy of Facebook adolescent–adult relationships for religious or spiritual development, Hodge (2010) has conducted a small study that reports online gamers experience their interactions as 'highly communal' and Morehead (2010) argues that 'cybersociality' is an example of an Oldenburgian 'third place': a public setting 'that host[s] the regular, voluntary, informal, and happily anticipated gatherings of individuals beyond the realms of home and work.' Thus, we cannot dismiss the potential for and likelihood that social networking contributes positively to the adolescent quest for connection.

Yet, we also cannot help but wonder whether the Facebook phenomenon might also be – or risk becoming – a form of pseudo-spirituality: a phenomenon which disguises itself as authentic spirituality, but which is actually and ultimately destructive and venomous. Berryman (2001) writes about pseudo-play as a deceitful representation which disguises itself as genuine play in order to lure people and then to suck from them their animating life force. In a similar way, the idea of pseudo-spirituality, while appearing as genuine, may in fact be deeply destructive.

Priestley (2002) maintains that the overall characteristic of the spiritual is that it is dynamic. Movement is of the essence. Pseudo-spirituality presents an outward showing of being dynamic. In relation to Facebook, spiritual dynamism may manifest in being able to communicate with several people at once from a myriad of different locations – not just in one city, but, if the participants are online at the same time, all over the world. Yet, each individual adolescent remains essentially isolated and bound to the computer, the lap top, or I-phone, each eagerly awaiting a reply to some comment posted on the recipient's wall. If a reply does not ensue, a sense of frustration and disconnectedness may be experienced or the young person may have to continue the search for others with whom to communicate. The Facebook user could become trapped when the anticipated dynamic connections he or she craves are met with static disinterest.

Priestley (2002) also argues that the spiritual may be described as being both personal and communal. While the personal element may be easily described in relation to cyber communication, the communal cannot so easily be determined. To what extent can a virtual community or an 'online community' be an authentic community? Does the twittering and strings and threads of an online discussion really lead to a sense of connectedness with Other, or does it effectually serve to remind those involved just how isolated they really are? This amounts to pseudo-spirituality. The promise of friends and conversation – the sense of connectedness with others – has the appearance of authenticity, but in reality, it may be a façade to mask the deep sense of loneliness experienced when one is sitting alone at the computer screen.

There is no question that social networking is a thriving adolescent activity. What we must ask is whether and how online phenomena such as Facebook and Twitter can be tools for and locations of spiritual development among the generation of digital natives currently caught up in a flurry of tweeting and posting, IM exchanges and photo sharing. Cyber spirituality or pseudo-spirituality? Without more study of and engagement with social networking practices, we just don't know.

References

Berryman, J.W. 2001. The nonverbal nature of spirituality and religious language. In *Spiritual education: Cultural, religious and social difference. New perspectives for the 21st century*, ed. J. Erricker, C. Ota, and C. Erricker, 9–21. Brighton, UK: Sussex Academic.

Ford, D. 1997. *The shape of living: Spiritual directions for everyday life.* Grand Rapids, MI: Baker Books.

Hodge, D. 2010. Role playing: Toward a theology of gamers. In *Halos and avatars: Playing video games with God,* ed. C. Detweiler, 163–75. Louisville, KY: Westminster John Knox Press.

Morehead, J. 2010. Cybersociality: Connecting fun to the play of God. In *Halos and avatars: Playing video games with God,* ed. C. Detweiler, 176–89. Louisville, KY: Westminster John Knox Press.

Priestley, J. 2002. The spiritual dimension of the curriculum: What are Ofsted inspectors looking for and how can we help them find it? Paper presented at the 3rd International Conference on Children's Spirituality, King Alfred's College, Winchester, UK.

Roehlkepartain, E., P. Benson, P. Scales, L. Kimball, and P. King. 2008. With their own voices: A global exploration of how today's young people experience and think about spiritual development. http://www.search-institute.org/csd/major-projects/with-their-ownvoices (accessed November 5, 2010)

Smith, C. 2009. *Souls in transition: The religious & spiritual lives of emerging adults.* New York: Oxford University Press.

Cyber spirituality II: virtual reality and spiritual exploration

Karen-Marie Yust, Brendan Hyde and Cathy Ota

Video gaming, whether online or via gaming systems, is a highly popular pastime for children and youth. Cartoon Network's New Generations surveys in the Philippines and India indicate that, of young people aged 7–14 with Internet access, 68% of Filipino children regularly participate in multi-player online games (Cartoon Network 2007) and 53% of Indian children identify multi-player or individual gaming as their favourite online activity (Demott 2010). An eight-year-old Nielson study of online gaming in Europe found that 12–24-year-olds are twice as likely to play online games as other age groups (Nielson 2003) and a more recent study in China reports that 8.1 million Chinese aged 25 years and under comprise one half the total number of Internet users in that country and cite online gaming as a top activity (Youth Mesh 2008). Among South Australian children, video game play comprises 19% of their multimedia time (Olds, Ridley, and Dollman 2006) and a Ministry of Education and Training survey in Vietnam 'showed 70 to 76 percent of primary school children play online games on weekdays' (CNN 2010). A Canadian study found that boys under 20 are more likely (80%) to play online games than girls in the same age group (20%) and that most play between 12 and 24 hours per week (Gladwell and Currie 2009). The most recent study released in the USA reports that children of 11–14 years old on average spend the most time playing video games each day (85 minutes), but all children aged 8–18 average more than an hour of daily gaming activity (Rideout, Foehr, and Roberts 2010).

Given this data, we cannot help but wonder how this gaming phenomenon affects the spiritual development of young people. In the fourteenth century, Catherine of Siena, a Christian mystic, reflected on the Eucharist and wrote, 'This food strengthens little or much, according to the desire of the recipient, whether he receives sacramentally or virtually' (Noffke 1980). By this she meant that attentive engagement in an imaginative act of partaking in a sacred ritual could have the same spiritual effect on a person as actual, physical participation in the ritual. Could this idea shape our reflections on contemporary children's participation in online and game box virtual realities?

The most popular online games (e.g. World of Warcraft, Halo, Ben 10, Toon Sports) are situated in fantasy. The players enter the game as characters participating in a 'hyper-real society' that invites them to escape the limitations of real life and take on experimental characteristics that may help them 'succeed' in ways they cannot otherwise achieve (Hodge 2010). Gaming storylines frequently adopt narratives of quest, apocalyptic threat, heroism and social action, which echo spiritual and religious concerns (Hodge 2010). Massively multi-player online role-playing games (MMPORGs) often involve the creation of avatars: virtual characters that embody aspects of the self a player wants to 'try on' or 'try out' in the virtual world of the game. The term 'avatar' comes from the Sanskrit and refers to the Hindu concept of a deity (most often Vishnu) that manifests in an incarnate (animal or human) form (Dictionary.com 2010). Inhabiting an alternative identity through an avatar can facilitate imaginative engagement in spiritual quests, battles between good and evil and challenges to prove their collaborative spirit and personal merit. Wagner (2010) suggests that young gamers may be empowered through the interactivity of the virtual quest to stretch themselves toward new identities and Hayse (2010) proposes that gaming can approximate a quest in the sense that it provides 'an education both as to the character of that which is sought and in self-knowledge' (40).

The virtual world is not without spiritual dangers, however. The Kids Help Phone study (Gladwell and Currie 2009) conducted online found that Canadian children overwhelmingly recognize the addictive potential of gaming and more than half of those responding believe gaming interferes with their school work and physical activities. A majority of the respondents who were worried about playing too much cited escapism as a major reason for their excessive gaming behaviour. One explained, 'It's easier to pretend you're someone amazing than to face the reality that you have issues. It's easier to make friends online who don't know you than to go out in the real world and let everyone see who you really are' (22). The Kaiser Family Foundation study in the United States (Rideout et al. 2010) revealed that young people who spend more than 16 hours a day consuming media-based content (including games) are more likely to feel sad, unhappy or bored with life. For these children and youth, participating in virtual realities inhibits rather than empowers their spiritual growth.

Significant questions remain, then, as to the long-term effects of regular participation in virtual reality games on children's spirituality. Given the ever increasing number of young people joining gaming ranks worldwide, we need studies that explicitly investigate the relationship between virtual quests and spiritual development so that we can identify and provide guidance for children's digital explorations of what it means to have meaning and purpose.

References

Cartoon Network. 2007. New generations briefing. Multiply. http://anikers.multiply.com/photos/album/21/Cartoon_Network_New_Generations_Briefing_21_November_2007

CNN Wire Staff. 2010. Vietnam restricts online gaming over youth concerns. Cable News Network. http://articles.cnn.com/2010-07-29/world/vietnam.online.gaming_1_online-games-gaming-companies-online-access?_s=PM:WORLD

DeMott, R. 2010. Cartoon Network to expand online games in India. Animation World Network. http://www.awn.com/news/internet-and-interactive/cartoon-network-expand-online-games-india

Dictionary.com Unabridged. 2010. 'avatar'. Dictionary.com LLC. http://dictionary.reference.com/browse/avatar

Gladwell, C., and J. Currie. 2009. Online gaming: Child's play or obsession? A Kids Help Phone Online Survey. Kids Help Phone. http://org.kidshelpphone.ca/media/53784/online% 20gaming%20 report%20 -%20english.pdf

Hayse, M. 2010. Ultima IV: Simulating the religious quest. In *Halos and avatars: Playing video games with God*, ed. C. Detweiler, 34–46. Louisville, KY: Westminster John Knox.

Hodge, D. 2010. Role playing: Toward a theology for gamers. In *Halos and avatars: Playing video games with God*, ed. C. Detweiler, 163–75. Louisville, KY: Westminster John Knox.

Nielson/NetRatings. 2003. Online gaming doubles in Europe in one year. Nielsen. http://www.nielsen-online.com/pr/pr030219uk.pdf

Noffke, S. 1980. Catherine of Siena: The dialogue. Mahwah, NJ: Paulist Press.

Olds, T., K. Ridley, and J. Dollman. 2006. Screenieboppers and extreme screenies: The place of screen time in the budgets of 10–13-year-old Australian children. *Australia & New Zealand Journal of Public Health* 30, no. 2: 137–42. National Center for Biotechnology Information. http://www.ncbi.nlm.nih.gov/pubmed/16681334?dopt=Abstract

Rideout, V., U. Foehr, and D. Roberts. 2010. Generation M2: Media in the lives of 8–18-year-olds. The Henry J. Kaiser Family Foundation. http://www.kff.org/entmedia/upload/8010.pdf

Wagner, R. 2010. The play is the thing: Interactivity from Bible fights. In *Halos and avatars: Playing video games with God,* ed. C. Detweiler, 47–62. Louisville, KY: Westminster John Knox.

Youth Mesh. 2008. The Phoenix generation: Insights into China's Youth. Pearl Research. https://www.youthmesh.org/wiki/index.php/China

Shining lights in unexpected corners: new angles on young children's spiritual development

Tony Eaude

ABSTRACT
In this article I consider how an inclusive understanding of young children's spiritual development can be enriched by research within the psychoanalytic tradition and cognitive psychology. I discuss difficulties of language and definition and suggest that thinking of spiritual experience as a type of experience rather than of spirituality or spiritual development may be helpful. Rather than working from a pre-determined definition, I argue that the meaning of spiritual experience is illuminated by considering a wide range of children's maturational and developmental needs and considering the boundaries of what may coherently be included as spiritual experience. In exploring research within these two traditions I suggest the integration of the personality as an end-point of spiritual experience which avoids a linear, upward idea of spiritual development. Finally, I consider the implications for research, about spiritual experience itself and for children and their teachers.

Introduction

In 1972, Hull (1998, p. 8) wrote 'Piaget's theory of the unfolding of intelligence is not adequate for religious growth. But from what source can Piaget be supplemented? We must look to psychoanalysis and to learning theory ...'. Although Piagetian notions of religious growth have been questioned, this challenge has been too rarely taken up to enrich new, and inclusive, understandings of young children's spirituality. In this paper, I explore some inherent difficulties in doing so, consider briefly the research approach adopted in my thesis (Eaude, 2002), suggest some promising areas within these disciplines and consider the wider implications.

My experience and interest lies with young children in ordinary schools rather than faith community settings. This is not to deny the importance of the latter but to assert that, unless spiritual development is the preserve of only some children, the most urgent issue is what can be done in the context of the school, as the public institution where almost all children attend. The tendency, often implicit, maybe even unconscious, of many commentators to conclude that children's needs are met only within a faith community does not address the reality that the vast majority of children in Western societies have no such link. By omission, presumably, these children are seen either to have no needs in this area or no way of these needs being addressed. I am searching for an inclusive understanding of spirituality, in the sense of referring both to all children and to the full range of children's needs and experience. Before losing those for whom spirituality is integrally linked with a framework of religious faith, I am not questioning the importance of religion—or that children's spirituality may flourish best within a faith tradition. But the most pressing issue is whether, and how, we can address the needs of the majority of children outside religious traditions. Given that spirituality is strongly rooted, historically, in religion and retains very strong associations with it, we need new ways of understanding children's spiritual development drawing on the insights both of religious traditions and of others less obviously associated with current perceptions of spirituality.

Clearing the Ground

The problem of definition, of what we mean by spirituality, confronts us at once. This goes beyond such familiar questions as the link between religion and spirituality, into the nature of meaning and language itself. It would be extremely useful to have a tight, clearly agreed, stipulative definition, universally accepted. But this is impossible. How we talk or write about such contested concepts both reflects and structures our understanding. This is further complicated by the underlying metaphors and connotations of which we may be aware only barely, or in some respects not at all. There is no common ground of agreement. Whatever we say about spirituality may always be open to the challenge 'but that's not spirituality, as I see it'.

Let me give a well-known example of how words both reflect and structure understanding. In using the term spiritual development, we commit ourselves in part to the assumption that children do develop spiritually. So our understanding of spirituality depends in part on our understanding of development. The notion of development as something incremental sits deep within us, tending towards a Piagetian view of sequential stages. Priestley (2000) explores the historical meaning of development, suggesting that its original—and in this context maybe more appropriate—meaning of unfolding has been distorted by its connotations in economics and to some extent psychology of a gradient of improvement, value, and end-product. However, the inappropriateness—or at least inadequacy—of this metaphor in this context is supported by religious traditions, which assert that children have specific qualities, which may be lost, or hard to re-gain, as adults, and that children provide models for adults to aspire to. At the very least, we need to understand children's spirituality as worthwhile in its own right, rather than as an immature or embryonic version of adult spirituality, however we see that. Priestley's suggestion of the metaphor of growth is better, but still, on its own, inadequate. We need, consciously, to adopt a range of metaphors, of health and of journey, as much as those of development and growth. Using only one set of metaphors traps us unduly in a limited and limiting language failing to do justice to the complexity of what is to be described.

In many ways, the term 'spirituality' poses similar problems. This has, for me at least, the connotation of being primarily interior and individual, based within a religious tradition. Yet what I seek to describe is something more basic, and wider, than religious faith or commitment, rather more akin to a universal search for meaning and identity. It relates more to the individual's place within culture, to values and relationships. While for many people this will involve a framework of religious faith and worship, for many others it will not. While we may more usefully talk of the spirituality of societies or cultures, to use the term 'spiritual experience' in relation to individuals seems to catch better that this is a type of experience, as one might talk of a puzzling or an enlightening experience. We cannot entirely avoid using a word like spirituality in common usage. Rather, we should attempt to examine and expose its underlying metaphors and presuppositions.

Although this may seem an insuperable barrier, it does not mean that we can say nothing about spirituality, rather that we need to operate within an unfamiliar, much more illustrative tradition. Symington (1986, p. 11) writes, explaining how to describe psychoanalysis, 'I am talking of a single reality but coming at it from different perspectives. This is the Hebrew rather than the Greek way of treating a human phenomenon. The Hebrew way is to go round and round a subject, each time using different images to illuminate what is most profound. The Greek way of arguing by logical stages can never, in my opinion, do justice to any deep experience.' Such an approach avoids the tendency to reductionism implicit in an approach based on exact definition. This reflects the inherently elusive and dynamic nature of spiritual experience, never quite to be pinned down. At best, we understand it obliquely, as through a glass darkly.

In my research, I approached children's spiritual development indirectly, by considering how fourteen teachers of four and five year olds in English primary schools understand this. I want to suggest how the research method adopted contributes to a wider understanding. I worked empirically to provide both a range of different viewpoints and a basis in practical activity rather than examining abstract concepts to find 'answers'. The problems of language outlined above make me suspicious of claims based on surveys, primarily because almost all of the terminology is contested, so that two similar responses may reflect quite different understandings. This can be, to some extent, circumvented by discussion but we are still faced with using words that lack a shared meaning, often without the differences being known to either party. To get at teachers' understanding, it is essential to see them at work, over a sustained period of time. The task is more in the nature of an ethnographic adventure, bringing into view the underlying aspects of teachers' beliefs buried in their practice by exploring what they do and say. Working with the teacher, as far as possible, as co-researcher, rather than as an object of study proved immensely fruitful. From the teachers' understanding I wished to draw out common features, recognising that there would be no consensus, and to highlight the dilemmas and tensions which inevitably occur in any understanding of what spiritual experience is and how the teachers resolved these.

My aim was, in seeing unprepared and casual responses, as well as more prepared ones, to explore the teachers' understanding within the rich context of teaching and to expose the underlying metaphors. To do this, I spent about eight days with each teacher to observe what happened in the classroom, with one discussion at the start, one after about five days and one at the end. This was designed to look at what they did more than what they said, but to draw insights from each and the interplay of the two. By seeing and discussing what actually happened and focusing on critical incidents and specific children, I hoped to draw out what they understood spiritual development to entail, rather than starting from a pre-determined definition.

Inevitably, as a researcher, one brings one's own understanding, and focuses on certain elements one associates with spiritual development. However, to understand the boundaries of contested concepts one needs to consider what is not within those boundaries as well as what is. I tried to consider the whole range of what the teachers did to explore what they understood spiritual development to involve. We illuminate what we mean by spirituality, or spiritual experience, by considering what we include and exclude. A good analogy is with moral development, where one would need to look both at what is explicitly deemed moral education and at the elements implicit in environments, ethos and relationships which contribute to moral development. However, to counter bias and projection, it is important both to make one's own presuppositions as explicit as possible and always open to challenge and not to use them as a rigid framework for the interpretation of the teachers' understanding.

Among the lessons learnt about this type of research are that:

- teachers were more able to recognise and describe spiritual experience by considering the familiar and practical context of the classroom, rather than dealing with abstract terms;
- indirect questions were often those that revealed most, for example, asking which aspects of the curriculum contributed least to spiritual development and what distinguished a spiritually mature or aware child from one seen as more generally mature; and
- asking why an activity did (or did not) contribute to spiritual development helped several teachers (and me) gain insight into their understanding more than to start with a predetermined set of activities deemed to be spiritual.

Inevitably, such research falls within the interpretative tradition. While one must be cautious about empirical claims, my work with teachers helped me to understand common features which they related explicitly to spiritual development and others which were implicit in how they taught. This is not to say that their views were to be taken at face value, nor that the majority view should hold more weight. The new understanding emerges from an interplay of historical traditions of spirituality, the teachers' understanding, demonstrated more in their teaching than in their words, and a range of research traditions which provide insight into young children both those explicitly related to spiritual development and others. In particular, it seems promising to consider how very young children develop, mature and learn. So, in taking up Hull's challenge, I consider what we may learn from the psychoanalytic tradition in the next section, and from cognitive psychology in the one after.

Exploring the Psychoanalytic Tradition

Particular strengths of the psychoanalytic tradition are the emphases on very close observation of young children, and on the centrality of emotion and role of pre-linguistic and unconscious influences. Early experience of emotion, and how this is processed, is seen to influence the personality profoundly. In many ways, Jung provides the source of inspiration for the research highlighted here. He argues that emotional wholeness entails getting in touch with symbolic meanings expressed in fantasy and that denial of these makes personal integration impossible. His emphasis on archetypes and the collective unconscious in how individual characteristics emerge resonates with Whitehead's insight (cited in Hay & Nye, 1998, p. 18) that one misconception about our understanding of our selves is the notion of independent existence. Jung provides the inspiration of Earl's (2001) work in describing the 'shadow' side of spirituality. I draw on these themes to suggest that a new understanding of spiritual experience can be formulated around the idea of integration of the personality.

Bowlby (1965) described the process of the child building a relationship with the prime-carer, almost invariably the mother, as attachment, establishing the link between mental well-being and the type of attachment formed. Secure attachment provides a good basis for personality development, and disorganised, anxious or avoidant attachment more unstable ones. While the pattern of attachment established in early infancy is not entirely unalterable later in life, it tends to persist. Winnicott's (1965, 1980) work builds significantly on Bowlby's in describing the conflicts of individuation and separation throughout early childhood, and beyond. The infant moves from a position of inability to distinguish between the self and others to a recognition that a world beyond exists, with which the emerging self can interact. Young (1994) draws on Winnicott in writing of 'potential space' as a (metaphorical) link between the internal world of the infant and external reality. This may be observed where an infant makes use of a 'transitional object', such as a small rag, or a toy, to act as a symbol with which to overcome the pain of the separation of the external world from the self. He describes how a 'holding' environment offers the emotional security and provides boundaries within which the exploration necessary for new learning to occur. While psychoanalysts use the term 'containment' in different ways, the child's anxiety must be contained, if it is not to inhibit maturation. Although most obvious in infancy, we never entirely lose the need for the space which Kimes Myers (1997, p. 63) describes as hospitable, 'the space in which old and new experiences are accepted, dealt with and transcended.' In his work on early childhood, Winnicott places great emphasis on the child making meaning through activity, and especially through play. He writes (1980, p. 63) 'it is in playing and only in playing that the individual child or adult is able to be creative and to use the whole personality. It is only in being creative that the individual discovers the self.' The learner needs to play, or at least to be playful, to try things out, to experience what newly constructed reality looks and feels like from within, managing the risk without bearing the consequences. As Loevinger (1987, p. 39) suggests, 'experience is mastered by actively repeating what one has passively undergone.' Making sense of experience requires the repeated re-visiting of difficult and disturbing experience, in safer, more contained situations. So the young child uses play to explore puzzling, unsettling and painful experience, without the danger of reliving the emotion. To explore the world beyond consciousness requires relatively risk-free environments. The world of play provides an opportunity for potential or hospitable space, for the worlds of illusion and reality, of consciousness and the extra-conscious to be safely explored.

The importance of the ego presents us with a paradox. Young children need to develop a strong, secure sense of ego, of selfhood, built on early attachment. However, an emphasis on our own needs to the exclusion of others restricts and diminishes us. Any observation of young children indicates how taken up they often are with their own immediate emotional needs. Yet many traditions of spirituality emphasise the importance both of emptying, of letting go of our immediate and personal concerns and of children providing a model of simplicity which adults would do well to follow. In achieving certain aspects of maturity, adults lose some of the positive qualities which children show.

Two key issues, which illuminate what characterises experience as spiritual, are those of perspective and independence. Think for a moment why experiences of awe and wonder are important. The answer seems to be that they help us to gain, or regain, a sense of perspective. This may be, psychologically, in terms of moving from too great a dominance by the ego, or, religiously, recognising our place in a wider context. Unless we are able to move away from dominance by the ego, we lose a sense of perspective, of what matters in terms beyond our immediate, often over-insistent, concerns. Similarly, too great an emphasis on the self deflects us away from a recognition of our interdependence. The feminist tradition challenges the widely held assumption that independence and autonomy are necessarily the desirable end-points of maturity, with Gilligan (1982) suggesting that most women see interdependence and relationship as more important. Slee (2000, p. 8) writes 'whilst some of the women did speak of mystical or numinous experience, for most, spirituality was rooted firmly in the everyday, mundane world of work, relationships, home life and contact with others.' We become who we are by recognising our place in relation to other people, to the world around and beyond. In Fairbairn's phrase, cited by Storr (1988, p. 150), the final stage of emotional development is 'mature dependence'.

The psychoanalytic tradition has tended to emphasise maturation and integration as an individual, internal process. However, Erikson (1968, p. 23) writes 'we cannot separate personal growth and communal change, nor can we separate ... the identity crises in individual life and contemporary crises in historical development because the two help to define each other and are truly related to each other.' Kimes Myers extends this, writing (1997, p. 17) that 'identity has a location, the cultural context mediated by family, surrounding the child.' The search for meaning and integration takes place within, and depends on, culture. The individual does not develop in a void, but in relationship to others.

Storr's (1960) idea of the integration of the personality seems to have three particular strengths in relation to children's spiritual development. First, the integrated personality has no single template of, but rather a constant movement towards, or away from, integration, which reflects the paradoxical nature of development. Second, it is multi-faceted, so that it relates to many different types of experience. Third, the process of integration involves making sense of the relationship between the internal world of emotions and beliefs and the external world of confusing, only-partly-explicable, experience. However, we need to highlight two caveats. The first is to recognise the risk of accepting, or even imposing, potentially damaging or incomplete models of integration. Integration is, by definition, a good thing. No one could seriously regard disintegration, or fragmentation, as desirable. Yet, is someone who is content, but never speaks to other people, integrated? Is the sociable person who takes little account of the consequences of his actions, to be seen as integrated? More controversially, is integration into an abusive relationship, or destitution, integration at all? Appropriate integration necessarily relates to values individually and collectively espoused. The second caveat is to recognise that the meaning of integration will, inevitably, vary between cultures. For example, since the Enlightenment, western societies have tended to see it in individual terms. Integration would previously in Western societies, and still in many Eastern cultures, be based far more on appropriate involvement in groups.

At the heart of my understanding of spiritual experience is the search for identity and meaning; for answers to questions such as 'who am I? where do I fit in? why am I here?' This must involve addressing the 'shadow side', 'everything that the subject refuses to acknowledge about himself and (which) is always thrusting itself upon him directly or indirectly.' (Earl, 2001, p. 285) This provides a rationale for helping children to integrate rather than deny those elements of the personality that each person may not wish consciously to accept or to recognise. It also suggests the importance of helping children make sense of the existential, ultimately unanswerable questions of life, of birth and death, of pain and suffering, rather than simply for adults to suggest that that these do not affect young children or to offer answers which offer too tidy a conclusion. In the name of protecting children, we are likely to be avoiding the potentially painful emotions that such questions evoke in ourselves.

From this section, several themes emerge. The first is the centrality of relationships, not least because they provide the basis of where we 'fit in'. Integration may be seen as resulting in, and evidence by, interdependence and appropriate relationships. Second, integration is not simply intra-personal, but involves finding one's place within (though often in uneasy relationship with) social and cultural structures and environments. The school is an important forum for spiritual development, but teachers cannot, of course, 'do it all'. They can aid and enhance the search for integration and may compensate, but only in part, for troubles and crises of identity and meaning resulting from the child's other experiences. Third, spiritual experience is not just something peripheral or optional, an internal, emotional trip that deals only with what is comfortable and pleasant. It is concerned with those basic questions that we all need to try and answer, although they are questions which we, and others, may not wish to address. I now move on to consider further insights from cognitive psychologists.

Learning from Cognitive Psychology

In this section, I extend the useful discussion started by Lewis (2000) to discover insights from cognitive psychologists who have tried to illuminate young children's spiritual development by looking at how they learn rather than simply to measure, empirically, what can be measured. In such contested areas, empirical work is of greatest value in helping us devise better frameworks of interpretation by exposing and challenging our own, and other people's, underlying presuppositions. Once again, we have to learn to live with uncertain and elusive boundaries in asking what, if anything, research into learning may tell us about children's spiritual experience.

Bruner (1986) suggests that, important though language is, there are prior, deeper, modes of learning. He delineates three modes, the enactive, the iconic and the symbolic (including language). Enactive learning, through, for instance, touch or mimicry, operates well before symbolic thinking appears. And iconic learning, through images, is again evident from very early childhood. Young children not only learn enactively and iconically, but they learn the earliest and profoundest lessons in these modes, especially in the affective domains. While the symbolic is in some senses the 'highest' of these modes, these are not Piagetian stages. Adults continue to learn in all three modes of learning, though the dominance of consciousness and language may make this hard to recognise. Think how language is often unable to cope with our responses to profound and unsettling experience; and our most deep-seated learning occurs at levels beyond or below that of language.

Young children are not blank templates on which adult patterns are etched. They are active participants in making meaning, agents in Bruner's terms, not simply passive recipients. This resonates strongly with the centrality of search in my description of spiritual experience. We grow and find meaning in life, and security, by understanding and solving problems, rather than having solutions or explanations imposed on us by others. Lambourn (1996, p. 153) highlights how identity is structured rather than given in writing 'I do not so much discover who I am, but rather choose who I am to be.' The constant re-creation of how we understand and describe reality leads Bruner (1996) to describe narrative as the medium for integrating individual learning into a wider system of thought and the individual into moral and thinking communities. The approach of exploring children's spirituality through their narratives as adopted by the Children and WorldViews Project (Erricker *et al.* 1997) seems a very appropriate way of exploring how children articulate their understanding of themselves.

Feldman's (1987) view of (conscious) learning is that pre-existing patterns of understanding remain in place, unless and until new experience unsettles them enough to enable the learner to create a new pattern assimilating the whole range of evidence, old and new. Patterns of understanding are re-shaped in the light of new experience which makes the previous pattern no longer adequate. This accords with Storr's (1960, p. 35) view that 'any form of new organisation or integration within the mind has to be preceded by some degree of disorganization. No one can tell, until he has experienced it, whether or not this necessary disruption of former patterns will be succeeded by something better.' Exploring questions and paradoxes arising from evidence and experience which conflict with existing understandings results in the formulation of new (but not final) resolutions. For young children, such shifts are more frequent than for adults because existing patterns are based on a narrower range of experience.

It is hard to escape the Piagetian framework of sequential, incremental stages of learning. In many areas of children's learning, his interpretative framework fits extremely well. However, Donaldson's (1984, 1993) research modifies Piaget's significantly, suggesting not so much that it is wrong but that it is inadequate in certain important respects. She suggests that, even in intellectual development, the level and nature of young children's responses are very context-related. Affective development is even more complex and situational. Donaldson's detailed description of various 'modes' as an alternative to the (serial) stages of Piaget and his followers is relevant in this context. Rather than a child moving from one stage to the next and (so to speak) discarding the previous approach, Donaldson sees new modes of understanding as an extension of repertoire rather than replacing the old. So infants experience the world initially in 'point-mode', move within a few months to 'line mode', and then into 'core-construct' mode, but maturity implies an increasing range of modes being available. To some extent, one may then able to choose which mode to apply, though this process is only partly conscious and controlled, as intense anxiety or fear, for example, may restrict the range available.

Claxton (1997) distinguishes between what he calls 'd-mode' thinking, which is 'conscious, deliberate, purposeful', and the slow ways of knowing including the intelligent unconscious, including such qualities as insight, intuition and wisdom. He argues (cited in Lewis, 2000, p. 274) that 'if we see d-mode as the only form of intelligence ... the lesson we learn from ... failures is that we must develop better models, collect more data, and ponder more carefully. We do not learn that we may have been thinking in the wrong way.' Claxton's appeal echoes Gardner's (1993) positing of a range of intelligences, rather than reliance on those, such as the linguistic and logical-mathematical, which tend to dominate our approach even where other intelligences may be more appropriate. In asking why ways of knowing other than d-mode are important, we see why space and reflection, and creative, imaginative activity, is so important in children's learning. These allow the unconscious to work and enable learning which is holistic, rather than encouraging only analytical approaches which break learning into constituent sections and skills. Over-reliance on one learning mode limits the range of the child's learning and fails to address adequately the more basic, but elusive, issues of meaning and identity.

Considering Wider Implications

I want to highlight three sorts of implication, about how to research children's spiritual experience, the nature of that experience and the consequences for children and their teachers. I believe that empirical studies based on quantification or (entirely) on what respondents say or write must be treated with caution and that, however time-consuming, observational studies provide a far more promising path. The approach which I adopted with teachers and their environment could be adapted for direct work with children, relying even more (than with teachers) on what they do than on what they say. The problem is that what one sees, and how one understands it, depends on the researcher's presuppositions—and these in turn, to some extent, determine the results. Three important ways of countering this seem to be to:

- make explicit the researcher's presuppositions, both initial and emerging;
- work in pairs or larger groups, so that similar incidents are seen and interpreted from differing perspectives; and
- learn to live with uncertain boundaries.

You may think that I have fallen into the trap that I warned against, of predetermining what I mean by spiritual experience and finding evidence within other disciplines to support this. In part, this is, inescapably, true, though my understanding of spiritual experience has become for me, much richer, in the search. Let me highlight three aspects emerging from this paper. First, although we probably have to live with the term spiritual development, this term does scant justice to the complexity and elusiveness of the subject. So, we need constantly and consciously to think of, and use, a range of metaphors. Second, although many areas of children's needs can usefully be separated into discrete areas, the spiritual overlaps with several other domains, including the emotional, the moral, the psychological. While, therefore, we need to see these categories as not mutually exclusive, what seems to underlie most views of spiritual experience—both religious and otherwise—is that it is a type of experience which deals with matters of significance, meaning and identity. Third, such experience, inevitably, has the potential to be painful as well as enriching, troubling as well as pleasant, both for the child and for the adult. So these are issues from which we may wish to protect both ourselves and our children—but which will re-appear, often in ways we find hard to bear, if they are not addressed. Spiritual experience helps us to gain, or re-gain, appropriate perspective which may be lost in the turmoil of busyness or anxiety, or the search for gratification or status.

Turning, finally, to the implications for schools, my experience is largely in English primary schools. However, current curricular trends in most school systems suggest that there are more widely applicable lessons to be learnt. As greater emphasis is placed on what can be assessed numerically, which is based on the assumption that all significant achievement is incremental, the range of curricular experience has narrowed. The way in which the curriculum, even for young children, has come to be conceived, planned and usually taught in subjects implies a view of learning heavily based on knowledge-acquisition with the teacher strongly in control of the agenda. Yet, this approach runs counter to the needs of the child indicated in the previous two sections, rather than seeing education as a two-way process and engagement. The challenge is to find ways of integrating children's experience rather than forever fragmenting it into discrete elements, of helping the child to respond to, and make sense of, (in the phrase of one teacher I worked with) 'moments of significance'. These, in their nature, cannot be predicted, and will vary from child to child, but the curriculum can enable, or inhibit, both their incidence and how children, and adults, respond when they do occur.

Of course schools, and teachers, must be concerned with the acquisition of skills and knowledge. But too great an emphasis on this, even for five and six year olds, in English schools at least, leads to an unbalanced curriculum which fails adequately to address the children's most important, but most elusive, needs. Let me offer a few examples. Although children have great capacity for curiosity and the questioning at the heart of making sense of experience, current approaches to pedagogy tend to over-determine the agenda and discourage children from making connections across disciplines. An over-full curriculum, with an insistent emphasis on pace and knowledge-acquisition, tends to deny opportunities for space and reflection. The same pressure has tended to reduce opportunities for children to experience stories, whether as hearer or as writer. While creative activity, such as music and art, provides for many people an especially important route into spiritual experience, the status of these two, and the time accorded to them, has reduced. The chance for children to play, and for drama, where, among other things, one can experience the world from a perspective other than one's own has similarly been squeezed out of the curriculum. Until the curriculum for young children draws more on the lessons of the psychoanalytic tradition and of learning theory, too many children will have insufficient opportunities in the search for meaning and identity—which, I suggest, is at the core of spiritual experience.

References

Bowlby, J. (1965) *Child Care and the Growth of Love* (London, Penguin).
Bruner, J. (1986) *Actual Minds, Possible Worlds* (Cambridge, MA, Harvard University Press).
Bruner, J. (1996) *The Culture of Education* (Cambridge, MA, Harvard University Press).
Claxton, G. (1997) *Hare Brain, Tortoise Mind: why intelligence increases when you think less* (London, Fourth Estate).
Donaldson, M. (1984) *Children's Minds* (London, Flamingo).
Donaldson, M. (1993) *Human Minds: an exploration* (London, Penguin).
Earl, M. (2001) Shadow and spirituality, *International Journal of Children's Spirituality*, 6(3), pp. 277–288.
Eaude, D. A. (2002) Beyond awe and wonder—a study of how teachers understand young children's spiritual development. D.Phil thesis, University of Oxford, available by contacting the author, as detailed above.
Erikson, E. (1968) *Identity: youth and crisis* (London, Faber & Faber). ERRICKER, C. et al. (1997) *The Education of the Whole Child* (London, Cassell).
Feldman, C. (1987) Thought from language: the linguistic construction of cognitive representations in: J. BRUNER & H. HASTE (Ed.) *Making Sense: the child's construction of the world* (London, Methuen).
Gardner, H. (1993) *Frames of mind: the theory of multiple intelligences* (London, Fontana).
Gilligan, C. (1982) *In a Different Voice* (Cambridge, MA, Harvard University Press).
Hay, D. & Nye, R. (1998) *The Spirit of the Child* (London, Fount).
Hull, J. (1998) *Utopian Whispers—Moral, Religious and Spiritual Values in Schools* (Norwich, Religious and Moral Education Press).
Kimes Myers, B. (1997) *Young Children and Spirituality* (London, Routledge).
Lambourn, D. (1996) 'Spiritual' minus 'personal-social' =?: a critical note on an empty category in: R. BEST (Ed.) *Education, Spirituality and the Whole Child* (London, Cassell).
Lewis, J. (2000) Spiritual education in the cultivation of qualities of the heart and mind: a reply to Blake and Carr, *Oxford Review of Education*, 26(2), pp. 263–283.
Loevinger, J. (1987) Paradigms of personality (New York, WH Freeman).
Priestley, J. (2000) Moral and spiritual growth in: J. MILLS & R MILLS (Eds) *Childhood Studies—A Reader in Perspectives of Childhood* (London, Routledge).
Slee, N. (2000) *A Subject in Her Own Right—The Religious Education of Women and Girls* (Hertford, Hockerill Educational Foundation).
Storr, A. (1960) *The Integrity of the Personality* (London, Heinemann).
Storr, A. (1988) *The School of Genius* (London, Andre Deutsch).
Symington, N. (1986) *The Analytic Experience* (London, Free Association Books).
Winnicott, D. (1965) *The Child, the Family and the Outside World* (Harmondsworth, Penguin).
Winnicott, D. (1980) *Playing and Reality* (Harmondsworth, Penguin).
Young, R. M. (1994) *Mental Space* (London, Process Press).

Index

Note: **Bold** page numbers refer to tables, *italic* page numbers refer to figures.

adolescent children: cyber spirituality 88–90
adult life 12, 14, 42, 61
adults' spirituality, life and journey 48
Allah 68
Allen, H.C. 20
Amey, A. 1
ancient civilisations 38
Andrews, C.R. 21
angels 37–39, 68
awareness sensing 13–14, 22

Batson, D. 15
Berger, P. 15
Berryman, J.W. 89
Bible 65, 68
big dreams 40
biological hypothesis: children's spirituality and metaphor 16; nature and nurture interact 17; spiritual education and social cohesion 16–17
Blake, W. 16
Bone, J. 24
Bosacki, S. 28
Bowlby, J. 98
Boyatzis, C. J. 28, 29
Bradburn, N. 12
Brailey, G. S. 4
Bray, Y. 4
Bronfenbrenner, U. 28
Bruner, J. 100, 101
Buddha achieved enlightenment 34
Buddhism and Thai Isan traditions 4
Busch, T. 54

Carr, D. 62
Carson, U. 54
Cartoon Network's New Generations surveys, Philippines 91
Catholic Church 49
Champagne, E. 25
Charlotte's web 54

child: development lab school 76, 77; imaginary friend 32; religious and/or spiritual concept 39; shade and protection 34; traditions and wider cultural influences 34
childhood education: early background 21; tablets 76
children: biological death 54; bipolar disorder 41; Christian tradition 38; divine dreams 38; dreams 40; encounters with angels 37–38; initiatory sessions 47; light and darkness shades 33–34; original and accessible framework 33; religious education 49; spiritual voice(s) 33; to symbols 34; in understanding death 48; and WorldViews Project 101
children's encounters 37
children's pragmatic descriptions 42
children's spaces 39
children's spiritual development 74; cognitive psychology 100–102; implication 102–103; incremental stages 101; psychoanalytic tradition 97–100; reflect and structure understanding 95–97; religious faith and worship 95; research method 96; risk-free environments 98
children's spiritual experiences: central metaphors 33–37, *35–37*; children's perceptions 41–43; interdisciplinary approaches 41; Jungian psychoanalytical approach 40; mental illness and religious 41; multidisciplinary approaches 40–41; nature 37–40; navigation tools 33, 37; relationship with traditions 37–40; spiritual space(s) 43–44; systematic studies 33
children's spirituality: agenda setting 16–17; an holistic awareness 10–11; biological interpretation 11–13; Bradburn balanced affect scale 12; in education 23–25; empirical research studies 19–21; findings and recommendations 27–29; Hardy's hypothesis 11–12, 16; identity formation

25–27; migration experience 3; multicultural approaches 28; musical or poetic sensitivity 10; non-religious and religious spirituality 20; pluricultural perspective 28; psychoanalysis 11; religious education 9–10; research methodology 20–21; secular culture **13,** 13–15; sense of self 25–27; spiritual care and spiritual needs 4; spiritual development 4; spiritual formation 4
children's (Christian) spirituality: children's voices 51–53; Christ's resurrection and the Christian belief 53; educational policy 23; faith education 56; interpretation 53–57; observations 48–51; spontaneity 51
children's spiritual spaces 45
children's spontaneity 51
children's voices: children's comments 53; children's spontaneity 51; recognising universality 52; sharing experiences 52; in their hearts 53
children's wisdom 48
child's life: integral component 84; spiritual experiences 32
Chow, W. 27
Christian: church 49; faith education 47; theology 13
Christian tradition 50; children 38; Paschal mystery and communication 50
Claxton, G. 102
Co-Evolution: Genes, Culture and Human Diversity (Durham) 17
Coleman, B. 26
Coles, R. 21, 62
Csikszentmihalyi, I. 14
Cumpsty, J. 15
cyber communication 90
cyber spirituality: Facebook 88–90; spiritual exploration 91–92; Twitter 88–90; virtual reality 91–92

Darcy-Berube, F. 54
dark spirituality 34, 43
Dawkins, R. 41
death and dying 48; children's comments 53; literature on children 53–54; stories and history 56–57
de Kock, A. 4
de Souza, M. 20, 43
devil 68
devotional life 66, 68, 69
Dewey, J. 82
disciples-accompagnateurs 48, 50, 51, 57
divine dreams 38–40
Donaldson, M. 14, 15, 22, 101
dreams 33; divine 38–40; psychological studies 39
Durkheim, E. 12
Durkheim's association: spiritual experience 12

Earl, M. 98
Eaude, T. 1, 26
education: Buddhist secondary schools 27; childhood education 25; educational policy 23; Life Orientation 23; South African teachers 24; teacher education programmes 23; therapeutic method 24
2011 Education Act 74
Eliade, M. 10
empirical research studies: children's spirituality 19–21; prominent themes 23; relationship to God 21–23; spiritual meaning-making 21–23
Erikson, E. 99
Erricker, C. 56, 63, 70
everyday life 65, 68, 69
evil 68, 91
Explique-moi la mort ... Guide pour accompagner l'enfant en famille et en catéchèse (Hofer) 54

Facebook 88–90; adolescent–adult relationships 89; adolescents *vs.* parents 89; messaging function 88; threads 89
faith journey 48
Feeling Good, Living Life (FGLL) 23
Feldman, C. 101
film 34
The Finnish religious education system: data and methods 64; DIT test 60; Finnish–Greek Orthodox Church 62; instrumentation 64; Lutheran church membership 63; Lutheran tradition 65; national curriculum 63; participants 64; Roman Catholic tradition 65; students' perceptions 64–69; three dimensions 66–69
Fisher, J.W. 23, 26
Fowler, J. 15
Freud, S. 12, 40

Gadd, A. 34
Gardner, H. 102
Gendlin, E. 14
Gilligan, C. 99
God 3, 4, 65, 68
Gomez, R. 26
Grande Halte: participants 50; phases 50; present children's reactions 48; socio-cultural issues 48
Guillebaud, J.-C. 55, 56
Gunnestad, A. 26

Hall, G.S. 9
Halstead, M. 83
Hardy, A. 10, 11
Hauerwas, S. 56
Haugen, H.M. 3
Hay, D. 12, 21, 25, 62

Hayse, M. 92
Hebrew Bible 39
history of religions 68
Hobson, J.A. 40
Hodge, D. 89
Hofer, M. 54
Holder, M. D. 26
Holy Spirit 48, 51
Hull, J. 94, 97
human being 16, 38, 47, 57, 69
human culture 69
the humanistic dimension 64, 66, 69
human life and culture 64; the humanistic dimension 64, 66
human nature: critical part 74
human spiritual journey 49
Hyde, B. 3, 4, 39
hyper-real society 91

individualism 15
Industrial Revolution 12
the institutional dimension 64, 66–69; sub-categories *67*, 67–68
International Journal of Children's Spirituality (IJCS) 1; editorial system 1; key themes or concepts 2, **2**
interpretation: an a-religious worldview 55–56; children's literature on death 53–54; and Christian spirituality 56; come and see 57; cultural ethos 55; risen community 57; stories and history 56–57; what happens after death? 55
invisible space 36–37, *37*, 43, 44
Islam 68
Islamic faiths 38

Jacobs, A. 23
James hypothesis: religious experience 9–10; spiritual experience 9
James theory 9
James, W. 9–11, 61
Jesus 47, 51–53, 55–57, 65
Joseph 51

The Kaiser Family Foundation study, United States 92
Kaiser, K. 4
Kallioniemi, A. 63
Karen-Marie, Y. 88
Kimble, C. 54
Kimes Myers, B. 98, 99
King David 51
Kool, B. 4

La force de conviction (Guillebaud) 55
Lambourn, D. 101
Leuba, J. 9

Lewis, J. 20, 62, 100
life and journey: adults' spirituality 48
Life Orientation (LO) 23
Lin, M. 4
living and dying: children's voices 51–53; interpretation 53–57; natural observation methodology 48–51
Livingston, J. 4
Loevinger, J. 98
Lucey, T.A. 4

Marotta, A. 21
Martin Luther 65, 69
Marx, K. 12
massively multi-player online role-playing games (MMPORGs) 91
Matthews, G.B. 48, 54
medical model 41
Melbourne Institute of Experiential and Creative Arts Therapy (MIECAT) 24
mental ill-health 41
mental illnesses 41
metaphors: border of darkness 34; invisible space 36–37, *37*; opaque space 36, *36*; positioning 34; shimmering space 35, *35*; spiritual dullness 34; vivid space 34–35, *35*
Ministry of Education and Training survey, Vietnam 91
Mister Rogers' Neighborhood (television show) 75
Mitchell, M.B. 22
Moore, K. 22, 28
Morehead, J. 89
Moriarty, M.W. 25
Morris, T. 5
Mountain, V. 24
Muslim 10, 39; *see also* Islam
Muslim children's dreams 39
mystery-sensing 14–15

National Core Curriculum for Basic Education (NCCBE) 63
natural observation methodology: the catechetical context 49–50; the participants 50; political and religious context 49; the programme 50–51
natural spirituality 10
nature and geography 69
navigation tools: children's spiritual experiences 33
Newcomb, J. 38
New England 9
Newton, I. 16
Nicodemus 51
Noddings, N. 63
non-religious spirituality 20
Nye, R. 21

opaque space 36, *36*
open-minded adult appears 43
Otto, R. 10, 14

Parker, S. D. 4
Parkinson, S. 4
personality disorders 41
Pettersen, A. 37, 43
The Philosophy of Childhood (Matthews) 54
Piaget's theory 94
Pimsa, W. 4
pluricultural approach
Potgieter, F. 39
preschool education: Neo-Confucian curriculum 5; settings 76; single-minded and reverential attention 5
Priestley, J. 89, 90, 95
psychotic disorder 41
Puolimatka, T. 63
Puritan society 9

Quran 39

Rankin, M. 42
Ratcliff, D. 21, 27, 29
religion and spirituality: common expressions 64–66, **65,** in Finnish school education 61–63; the humanistic dimension 66, 69; the institutional dimension 64, 66–68; multicultural world spirituality 61; nature and relationships 62; students' perceptions 64–69; the supernatural dimension 64, 67–68
religious education programmes 11, 39, 49; children's active participation 48; ethics and religious culture 49; in Finland 62; Finnish culture and education 62; global catechetical approach 49; primary level 62–63; primary responsibilities 63; school curriculum 62; secondary level 63
religious experience: biological interpretation 11; Durkheim's 'social effervescence' hypothesis 12; Freud's dismissal 12
religious settings 68
religious spirituality 20
religious traditions 68
research methodology 20–21; four salient phases 21; qualitative phenomenological study 21; search terms 20–21
Ricoeur, P. 16
Riegel, U. 4
Robinson, C. 3
Robinson, E. 21
Roehlkepartain, E.P. 88, 89
Rogers, F. 75
Roman Catholic 65, 68
Roman Catholic Church 69

Ross, C. J. 22
Rust, F.O. 1

Saint-Jean-Longueuil 47, 49
Satan 68
Saussure. F. de 10
Schleiermacher, F. 10
Schonfeld, D. 54
school: in Australia 23; child development lab 76; in Great Britain 21; interviewing elementary children 25; public elementary and secondary 49; religious education lesson 39; in South African 23
Schutz, A. 14
Scott, D.G. 43
Selznick, P. 17
Sewell, J. 4
shimmering space 35, *35,* 43
Silver, C. F. 22
single vision 16
Slee, N. 99
Smith, C. 89
social cohesion 16–17
social-ecological model 28
spiritual child: creative energy 81–82; naturist and visionary 80–81; transformative education empowers 82–83; wonder childhood moments 78–79
spiritual education 16–17
spiritual experience 9; Durkheim's association 12; Gallup Omnibus Survey 12
spirituality: research question and methodology 76–77; role 73–74; spiritual awareness 77; teachers' supporting role 77–78; and technology 74–75; technology tools 75–76; wonder childhood moments 78–79; young children 74
spiritual sensitivity: awareness sensing 13–14; awareness-sensing 22; inter-related themes or categories **13,** 13–15; mystery-sensing 22; mystery-sensing 14–15; value-sensing 22; value-sensing 15
spiritual space(s) 42, 43–44
Spiritual Support and Community Involvement Service 49
spiritual well-being (SWB) 23
spiritual well-being questionnaire (SWBQ) 26
Starbuck, E.D. 9, 11
St-Gelais, R. 49
Stifoss-Hanssen, H. 66
Storr, A. 99, 101
Suber, M. 15
supernatural actions 68
the supernatural dimension 64, 67–69
Surr, J. 3

SWBQ *see* spiritual well-being questionnaire (SWBQ)
Symington, N. 96

tablets and technology: children's fascination 84; digital citizenship 75; digital games 75; nature neurons 81; outdoor photographs 80; spiritual awareness 77; and spirituality 74–75; supporting and empowering spiritual tool 75–76; teachers' supporting role 77–78; video gaming 91
Talwar, V. 28
Tamminen, K. 13
Tan, C. 5
Tangvoraphonkchai, J. 4
teacher education programmes 23
Thanattheerakul, C. 4
Thwala, S'I. 26
Tirri, K. 60, 63
transcendence 68
Troeltsch, E. 10
Tuck everlasting 54
Twitter 88–90

Underhill, J. 38

value-sensing 15
van der Walt, J. L. 39
The Varieties of Religious Experience (James) 9

video games 34; Filipino children 91; Indian children 91; multi-player online games 91; online games 91; South Australian children 91
virtual world: games 91; kids help phone study 92
vivid space 34–35, *35,* 38, 40, 42, 44

Wach, J. 10
Wagner, R. 92
Waite, S. 83
Wallace, J. 26
Watson, J. 3, 5
western Christianity 70
Wills, S. 25
Winnicott, D. 98
Wolhuter, C. C. 39
Wordsworth, W. 12
World Health Organization (WHO) 2
Wu, S. 5

Yeung, G. K. K. 27
young children: behaviours 74; preschool educational settings 76; spirituality 74
Young, R.M. 98
Yust, K. M. 3

Zhu Xi 5
Zinnbauer, B. 61, 68